THE
PREFACES
OF
HENRY JAMES

JOHN H. PEARSON

THE
PREFACES
OF
HENRY JAMES

Framing the Modern Reader

The Pennsylvania State University Press
University Park, Pennsylvania

Library of Congress Cataloging-in-Publication Data

Pearson, John H., 1955–
    The prefaces of Henry James : framing the modern reader / John H. Pearson.
      p.   cm.
    Includes bibliographical references (p.   ) and index.
    ISBN 0-271-01659-0 (alk. paper)
    1. James, Henry, 1843–1916—Technique.   2. Fiction—History and criticism—
Theory, etc.   3. Modernism (Literature)—United States.   4. Authors
and readers—United States.   5. Reader-response criticism.   6. Narration
(Rhetoric).   7. Fiction—Technique.   8. Prefaces.   I. Title.
PS2127.T4P43   1997
813'.4—dc20   96-31044
                                                          CIP

It is the policy of The Pennsylvania State University Press to use acid-free paper for
the first printing of all clothbound books. Publications on uncoated stock satisfy the
minimum requirements of American National Standard for Information Sciences—
Permanence of Paper for Printed Library Materials, ANSI Z39.48—1992.

CONTENTS

for Rowan and Elly

ACKNOWLEDGMENTS

This study was long in the making, and would not have been possible except for the help of many friends and colleagues. Like James, I find myself in my revisionary tour of the manuscript surrounded by memories of those who contributed what often seems the greater share of the work. When I began this project, Millicent Bell, John T. Matthews, Susan Mizruchi, Michael McKeon, Carolyn Williams, William Vance, Helen Vendler, and Bonnie Costello offered invaluable advice, assistance, and encouragement. I am especially indebted to David McWhirter for his continued and extraordinary support of this work, including his thoughtful, intelligent suggestions for revision. I received financial support from Boston University and Stetson University: the Boston University fellowship enabled me to conduct research and begin the first draft of the manuscript; a grant from Stetson University allowed me to complete that task, and for those opportunities I am equally thankful. I am grateful for permission to print revisions of my article "The Politics of Framing in the Late Nineteenth Century," *Mosaic* 23 (Winter 1990): 15–30, which appear in Chapter 2. Finally, I must acknowledge the two individuals who have had the most profound effects on this book and on my life while I wrote it. Keith Baber was an extraordinary friend during the early stages of my work. And to Terri Witek, I owe nothing less than this work itself: without her support, critical acuity, and encouragement, these pages would be thwarted ambition.

INTRODUCTION

In the first decade of the twentieth century, Henry James found himself putting together an edition of his novels and tales that conjured images of exaltation and death. He likened himself to Ozymandias, hoping for acknowledgment of his great achievement as a novelist, yet fearing that the New York Edition would become nothing more than a shattered monument to an inflated ego. In either case, the edition that would represent his life's work could be conceived only by acknowledging that the life and its work were coming to an end. In fact, when first contemplating the project, James called the similar enterprise of his contemporary Paul Bourget, a marble "mosaic sarcophagus."[1] The author once canonized is sealed in a tomb. If James's passion was for appreciation and discrimination of his works in the large European and American literary marketplace, as he told William Dean Howells, then his task as creator of the New York Edition was to construct a tome, not a tomb, that would ensure the creation and maintenance of Jamesian readers. The New York Edition must not only be the product that represented James on the marketplace; it had to carry the burden of creating desire for its own consumption.

1. Quoted in Leon Edel, *Henry James: The Master; 1901–1916* (Philadelphia: Lippincott, 1972), 321. All references to the New York Edition and its prefaces are to Henry James, *The Selected Novels and Tales of Henry James*, 24 vols. (New York: Charles Scribner's Sons, 1906–8).

The prefaces to the New York Edition became the ground on which James worked to create this desire. There James would invent the critical apparatus, as R. P. Blackmur notes in his introduction to *The Art of the Novel*, by which his novels and tales could be understood—would be appreciated, that is, in just the way James hoped. The following study examines the strategies that James employs in the eighteen prefaces to prepare the reader for the prefaced texts. I argue that James created the modern reader, largely accomplishing what Blackmur claims he set out to do, by assuming authority over his work both as its creator and ideal consumer, and then overtly and covertly instructing his readers how to appreciate and discriminate Jamesian literary art.

My argument begins with a consideration of James's motives for attempting to colonize, as I claim, a segment of the literary marketplace. Rather than adapt his art to suit the prevailing desires of the market, James stood firm in his devotion to his aesthetic of fiction and sought instead to create desire. The problem became a formal one: on the one hand, James must guard the integrity of his novels and tales by maintaining their formal boundaries and remaining as literary guide outside the house of fiction; on the other, he would position himself close enough to those texts to guide the reader through them. He could lead his reader to the threshold of the house of fiction, in other words, but he could not risk being detected inside; that would destroy the effect of the fictive world and of the art itself. The first chapter of the present study offers some theoretical background for James's use of the preface to position himself at the lintel of his aesthetic world. The prefaces act in many respects as literary frames in this regard, as James relies upon a long tradition of framing in the literary and plastic arts to develop strategies for achieving his ends. The second chapter describes this tradition, identifying analogues and antecedents for James's strategies for creating the ideal reader through the aegis of the frame.

The remainder of this study examines those strategies. First, James must claim authority over the novels and tales. He does this through the tales of origin that begin nearly every preface. James claims a unique relationship to the works of fiction: while reading them over for revision and republication, he detects signs of their origins and development. These narrative histories are James's alone to tell, and he establishes his authority over his own work by uniting his work as creator and ideal reader of his fiction. He then poses as a model reader, discovering value here and an occasional literary problem there. In Chapter 3, through readings of the prefaces to *The Awkward Age* and *The Aspern Papers*, I demonstrate the intricate pattern that James establishes through the tales of origin, connecting the readers to the author-turned-ideal-reader, and finally to James's idealized reading of those novels.

James further prepares his readers by supplementing his novels and tales with criticism of their methods, of specific scenes, and of the various choices that the author made while writing. James frequently presents himself as the heroic artist struggling with complex literary problems and obstacles, and in so doing encourages his reader to attend to authorial performance. The novels and tales then become illustrations of the artist's method and achievement as well as works of art. In Chapter 4, I contend, however, that James was attempting to supplement the reader through these previews of the text rather than to augment the texts themselves. According to Derrida's theory of supplementarity, the supplement always gestures toward some absence or lack in that which is supplemented. If the prefaces add to the texts that they precede, then they are clear indications that those texts are not complete, are not fully present, and are therefore in need of such supplementation. This was not James's contention. Instead, and as his decision to create a readership rather than to appease the present one indicates, James believed that the readership needed supplementation. My readings of the prefaces to *The Wings of the Dove* and *What Maisie Knew* explain how James attempts to supplement his reader, and in the process how he throws light onto his own authorial performance.

This study repeatedly gestures toward many issues in semiotic theory. Its consideration of the preface as a frame alone incites interartistic debate. Chapter 5 returns to this debate as it considers those volumes of the Edition that contain several tales. The prefaces to those volumes must somehow frame several texts, and implicitly, I argue, must enleague those texts as various examples of authorial performance. The preface to volume 17, which contains many of James's best-known ghost stories, brings those tales as well as "The Altar of the Dead," "Beast in the Jungle," and "The Birthplace" into a complex semiotic field that is bordered and in fact created by the volume itself and, most important, by its preface. The preface defines the terms of that field, and surprisingly to those who would seek there a description of James's method of horror and suspense, we find a rather prolonged consideration of the economic histories of the longer stories, with deeply felt expressions of frustration at the apparently divergent economic and aesthetic values of those texts. In this preface, and then through the idealized reading of the prefaced tales, James asks his reader to address the very pressing question of value as it is determined in the literary marketplace.

The tales become transformed in this light as allegories of aesthetic value and the conflict of values inherent in the early twentieth century.

In the final chapter I show briefly how these strategies work together to facilitate a reading of *The Portrait of a Lady* that would be validated by the author himself. Rather than discover some new insight, I instead attempt to show that the many standard readings we have come to accept are all prescribed by the author. They are latent in the preface, which itself is something of a meditation on consciousness as the vehicle through which everything is known and through which the self is constructed. That concept is central to James studies, as Dorothea Krook's *The Ordeal of Consciousness* first and best argues. The implications are important to the present study because James desired his readers to be conscious not only of the value of his art, but of the value of his aesthetic performance. We must always read novel and novelist, in other words. That is the great desire that informs the architecture of Henry James's New York Edition of his novels and tales.

Colonizing the Reader:
The New York Edition's Architecture of Desire

When Henry James began working on the proposed edition of his collected novels and tales, he wrote to his editor at Charles Scribner's Sons that he "should particularly like to call it the New York Edition if that may pass for a general title of sufficient dignity and distinctness." Apparently James wanted to give an American cast to the literary monument, to refer "the whole enterprise," he explained, "to my native city," making New York (and America) a frame of reference that has been little understood or considered.[2] Ironically, the New York to which James and the Edition refer is not the New York that James had recently visited. Writing about the prodigal journey to America that he made after a twenty-year absence, James concluded that America in general and New York City in particular were not the same places that he had left as a young, aspiring novelist for what he felt certain would be the aesthetically richer milieux of Britain and Europe. The "family-party smallness of the old New York," James laments in his autobiography, had become "a vision of energy," a "monster [that]

2. Quoted in Edel, *Master*, 321.

grows and grows, flinging abroad its loose limbs even as some unmannered young giant."[3] Although James would renounce his American citizenship a few years later, in 1907 he sought to identify his magnum opus by naming it after his place of origin—a place that no longer existed except in the author's memory and, therefore, as an originating frame of reference for the author's identity. James wanted to collect and compose his novels and tales, that is, within a foremost frame—the name inscribed on the Edition—that recalls the beginning of authorial consciousness and not the city of New York per se.[4] This is the first mark on the New York Edition that suggests, though obliquely, James's desire to transform his fiction into self-conscious works of art that refer to the aesthetic powers of their creator. Such reference (and deference) is part of James's rigorous effort to demark the Edition as the totem that spiritualizes its author.

Quentin Anderson has offered the most prolonged examination of this anamoly. In another ironic twist that belies that collection's name, Anderson notes, the New York Edition contains almost no stories of New York, America, or the New World. James omitted *Washington Place* and *The Europeans*, for example, partly for practical purposes, but primarily because these works would not help him achieve his goal: James omitted his American stories and tales in an effort to woo American readers by carrying European culture "home in triumph."[5] Through the New York Edition, Anderson argues, James attempts to exercise his nascent imperialism, which is utterly American (the tradition of Emerson and Whitman) yet is for James central to his experience of Europe. Repeatedly in the narratives of the Edition, James "conquers the great world of European culture and art" by subjecting it to, and possessing it through, his fiction. This argument enables Anderson to resolve the conflict between the American label on the Edition and James's decision to omit most of his American novels and tales from it. In this sense,

3. Henry James, *Autobiography: A Small Boy and Others; Notes of a Son and Brother; The Middle Years*, ed. Frederick W. Dupee (Princeton: Princeton University Press, n.d.), 158; *The American Scene* (Bloomington: Indiana University Press, 1968), 79.

4. David McWhirter agrees that "James's decision to name the edition after his native city . . . unquestionably evokes the authority of origins"; however, the decision also suggests to McWhirter, in light of his reading of *The American Scene*, that James recognized "that his quest for an authoritative, monumental permanence has resulted instead in a 'wondrous adventure' of ever-unfolding difference." "(Re)Presenting Henry James: Authority and Intertextuality in the New York Edition," *Henry James Review* 12 (1991): 140.

5. Quentin Anderson, *The Imperial Self: An Essay in American Literary and Cultural History* (New York: Knopf, 1971), 167.

Anderson too sees the Edition as James's totem, for its aesthetic conquest of Europe ultimately reflects upon the conquering hero—its author. Yet for James, the triumphant homecoming enacted in the Edition was anything but satisfying because, metaphorically speaking, no one came to welcome him.[6] During his career, James never developed a sizable readership in America, and the changes in American culture evident to James during his prodigal tour at the beginning of the century suggested a reason why he was so poorly received. His purported compatriots no longer adhered to the standards and values upon which so much of upper-class nineteenth-century American life, including James's, was built. His fictive worlds reflect those values. Yet they also reflect notions of identity and consciousness that are distinctly modern, as successfully argued by both John Carlos Rowe in *Henry Adams and Henry James: The Emergence of Modern Consciousness* and Ross Posnock in *The Trial of Curiosity: Henry James, William James, and the Challenge of Modernity*. Posnock claims that in the first decade of the twentieth century, James was engaged in a "personal project [which] both echoes and anticipates the concerns of American and European cultural criticism": "the philosophical oppositon to identity logic," or what we have come to recognize in modern literature as the notion of an inessential self (81).

To a great extent, James was successful in his attempt to create a modern, distinctly Jamesian reader. As Hershel Parker has recently argued, the prefaces, best known in and as Blackmur's *The Art of the Novel*, have "tyrannized over criticism on Henry James." Parker's history of critical responses to the prefaces reveals a long and empowered tradition that takes the prefaces as highly privileged and coherent critical discourse. For example, while Laurence Holland, one of James's best readers, considers the prefaces a "celebration of a process, a mission, and a form rather than a statement of theory," he, like most of James's readers in the last ninety years, defers to the prefaces.[7]

---

6. In a letter to Edmund Gosse (August 25, 1915), James admitted that the Edition was "a complete failure," which he explained, saying that "vulgarly speaking, it doesn't sell. . . . I remain at my age (which you know), and after my long career, utterly, unsurmountably, unsaleable." *Henry James Letters*, vol. 4, ed. Leon Edel (Cambridge: Harvard University Press, 1984). Miranda Seymour argues that "it was, above all, the terrible sense of failure represented by the unsaleability of the New York Edition which haunted [James] and preyed on his mind and which, sadly, . . . reduced him to a sobbing and hysterical invalid." *A Ring of Conspirators: Henry James and His Literary Circle, 1895–1915* (Boston: Houghton Mifflin, 1989).

7. Hershel Parker, "Deconstructing *The Art of the Novel* and Liberating James's Prefaces," *Henry James Review* 14 (1993): 285; Laurence Bedwell Holland, *The Expense of Vision: Essays on the Craft of Henry James* (Baltimore: Johns Hopkins University Press, 1964), 156.

The most recent project to address James's New York Edition and its prefaces is a collection of essays that for the first time considers the Edition as a construction of authorship. In *Henry James's New York Edition: The Construction of Authorship*, David McWhirter and Paul B. Armstrong contribute important interventions in the critical discourse about James's intentions and methods in the prefaces, especially as those intentions regard James's notion of the ideal reader. McWhirter notes the important contradiction inherent in James's enterprise: "For if the Edition can be seen as an attempt at monolithic self-definition, it also should be apprehended as a conscious experiment in intertextuality which deliberately brings a variety of different 'voices'—the original texts, the revisions, the prefaces, the frontispieces . . . —into relations, without insisting that they converge on any architectural or monumental completeness."[8] I argue here that they do indeed converge, first in the author's performative consciousness as it is manifested in the prefaces, and then in the consciousness of the reader indoctrinated by those prefaces—the modern reader that James sought avidly to create and protect. This is the argument made by Paul B. Armstrong: "A case can be made, I think, that the strangeness of these introductions [the prefaces] is useful, justifiable, and perhaps even intentional. James is aware through the prefaces of the need to educate the readers to the ideal of criticism he finds lacking in his world." In fact, Armstrong contends, the prefaces "provide the reader with a hermeneutic education that simulates modes of understanding appropriate for construing his fiction." The prefaces produce a reader with the requisite discipline "to attend rigorously and carefully to meanings not their own"— to meanings authorized in the prefaces themselves and carried forward into the novels and tales of the Edition.[9] In her essay "Shame and Performativity: Henry James's New York Edition Prefaces," Eve Kosofsky Sedgwick considers James's emphasis on authorial performance in the prefaces. Sedgwick offers one of the first comprehensive analyses of the rhetoric of the prefaces, suggesting that these texts are the products of James's almost desperate desire for validation.[10] Sedgwick clearly breaks with the tradition of readers

8. David McWhirter, " 'The Whole Chain of Relation and Responsibility': Henry James and the New York Edition," in *Henry James's New York Edition: The Construction of Authorship*, ed. David McWhirter (Stanford: Stanford University Press, 1995), 7.

9. Paul B. Armstrong, "Reading James's Prefaces and Reading James," in *Henry James's New York Edition: The Construction of Authorship*, ed. David McWhirter (Stanford: Stanford University Press, 1995), 131, 133.

10. Eve Kosofsky Sedgwick, "Shame and Performativity: Henry James's New York Edition Prefaces," in *Henry James's New York Edition: The Construction of Authorship*, ed. David McWhirter (Stanford: Stanford University Press, 1995), 206–39.

inaugurated by James himself that have taken the prefaces as nearly sacred critical texts upon which hermeneutical authority rests, and subjected them to the same scrutiny that the literature itself deserves.

As the several critical essays in *Henry James's New York Edition* suggest, the Edition was a project generated by personal and professional conflict. James would create a monument to fix his identity as author, yet he increasingly suspected the notion of a fixed identity. He would recall readers to an earlier time when his values were more in tune with the world about him, yet he would propel both his readers and his work into an uncertain future where he hoped to be canonized. Most poignantly, James would make the New York Edition definitive, and thereby write himself out of work by signaling the end of his career, as a means of enlivening his career and enriching his purse.

For the New York Edition of his works to be definitive—and James Pinker, James's agent, explained to Edward Burlingame, the senior editor of Charles Scribner's Sons, that this was James's goal—his works must be fully and finally complete, no longer in need of the artist's refining touch or other authorial enterprise. Therefore, the work that would represent James in the literary world for generations to come—and particularly in the literary marketplace—would be the work that relegated James to the past. Although the Edition would immortalize him as a formidable literary figure, the project itself would inevitably signify the end of James's literary career.[11] The distinct implications accompanying the creation of his own mosaic sarcophagus define sharply the image of James aggressively trying to determine and control its reception, first by revising the texts.[12] This implies that James was engaged in both an admission of and a struggle against his (authorial) mortality. In fact, he characterizes himself in the early stages of his work on the New York Edition as a reader (of his own work) who by necessity must become the resurrected if not ghoulish author:

> I find this ghostly interest [constructing the Edition] perhaps even
> more reasserted for me by the questions begotten within the very

11. As Michel Foucault notes, this realization of what has come to be known as the death of the author is fundamental to authorial identity: "Writing has become linked to sacrifice, even to the sacrifice of life: it is now a voluntary effacement which does not need to be represented in books, since it is brought about in the writer's very existence." "What Is an Author?" in *The Foucault Reader*, ed. Paul Rabinow (New York: Pantheon Books, 1984), 102.

12. Walter Benn Michaels argues that for James *rewriting* is *rereading*. See "Writers Reading: James and Eliot," *Modern Language Notes* 91 (1976): 827–49.

covers of the book, those that wander and idle there as in some sweet old overtangled walled garden, a safe paradise of self-criticism. Here it is that if there be air for it to breathe at all, the critical question swarms, and here it is, in particular, that one of the happy hours of the painter's long day may strike. I speak of the painter in general and of his relation to the old picture, the work of his hand, that has been lost to sight and that, when found again, is put back on the easel for measure of what time and the weather may, in the interval, have done to it. Has it too fatally faded, has it blackened or "sunk," or otherwise abdicated, or has it only, blest thought, strengthened, for its allotted duration, and taken up, in its degree, poor dear brave thing, some shade of the all appreciable, yet all indescribable grace that we know as pictorial "tone"? The anxious artist has to wipe it over, in the first place, to see; he has to "clean it up," say, or to varnish it anew, or at the least to place it in a light, for any right judgement of its aspect or its worth. (1:xii)

James first experiences his older work—in this case, *Roderick Hudson*—as if he were a passive but secure reader, someone entangled in an "overgrown" but superficially safe environment that at times sounds eerily like a grave. James's diction and metaphor are revealing in this regard: "ghostly," "if there be air for it to breathe at all," "has been lost to sight," and perhaps most graphic of all, "Has it too fatally faded, has it blackened or 'sunk' "? Has the work of art, in other words, not been properly mummified and protected within its marble sarcophagus? The act of reading his own work, as if he were James's legatee or mourner rather than the author himself, allows James to assume a stance from which he may engage in criticism (self-criticism), and so the author is fully empathic toward his reader. At this point James is fully engaged in a double vision as reader and writer.[13] When this double vision approves of the work, reader and writer momentarily merge, whereupon James happily discovers "the artist, the prime creator";

---

13. This double vision has been referred to variously by recent critics. John Carlos Rowe refers to the "two Jameses—the James of Experience and the James of Form—[who] represent a doubleness in his theory of the novel." *Theoretical Dimensions of Henry James* (Madison: University of Wisconsin Press, 1984), 229. David Carroll argues that there are "two 'I's' (eyes) at the heart of James's theory of point of view. . . . As one eye is fixed in its place, focusing on and determining the unity of form, the other eye, not quite in focus, barely glimpses at (wonders at) the complex conditions dividing, interfering with, and complicating that unity." *The Subject in Question: The Language of Theory and the Strategies of Fiction* (London: University of London Press, 1982), 66.

this discovery provides the reading writer a highly privileged, almost sacred knowledge of the text that resurrects "the dead reasons of things, buried as they are in the texture of the work, and makes them revive, so that the actual appearances and the old motives fall together once more, and a lesson and a moral and a consecrating final light are somehow disengaged" (1:xii). In other words, this ghostly interest allows James to step back in time, to become rejuvenated as the author confronting his great passion, his task. Yet this immortality is illusory: upon completion of his ghostly interest, James will be forced to release his grip on the work and foreswear further rereadings and revisions, leaving it with the world in uncertain hope of "right judgement of its aspect or its worth." This eternal separation from his work saddened James: "We are condemned," he says in the final preface, " . . . whether we will or no, to abandon and outlive, to forget and disown and hand over to desolation, many vital or social performances—if only because the traces, records, connexions, the very memorials we would fain preserve, are practically impossible to rescue for that purpose from the general mixture" (23:xx). With this, James acknowledges that revision is inadequate to the tasks of controlling reading and, most poignantly, controlling the passing of time. James's noble aesthetic purpose is threatened by the inclusive and often confusing general mixture that is the extraliterary world—the world of the unindoctrinated reader and of time, which will not be subjugated to any individual's aesthetic vision. He could neither abandon or outlive his aesthetic vision; yet completion of the project would bring an end to his social *cum* literary performances and lead to authorial extinction of a very real kind.

James's hope, therefore, like Lear long before him, was to find solace in the assurance of total devotion of his progeny. The sense of urgency with which James encounters his reader erupts in the framing prefaces, rendering them sometimes aggressive, sometimes unstable, and always conflicted texts. This conflict is endemic to the relationship between writing and authorial death, a relationship particularly resonant in a project that seeks to provide definitive shape to the concretions of one man's literary imagination. Foucault explains that "the relationship between writing and death is . . . manifested in the effacement of the writing subject's individual characteristics. Using all the contrivances that he sets up between himself and what he writes, the writing subject cancels out the signs of his particular individuality. As a result, the mark of the writer is reduced to nothing more than the singularity of his absence; he must assume the role of the dead man in the game of writing."[14] The general condition of the author that Foucault describes is the particular condition of the realist writer, who believed him- or herself ideally a transparent and catalytic vehicle for the literary intersubjective presentation of the world. James felt his authorial absence in the text acutely. As he read his revised work one last time before writing each preface, he discovered himself as a reader "in the presence of some such recording scroll or engraved commemorative table—from which the 'private' character . . . quite insists on dropping out" (1:v). But James was not ready to let go or be left behind. Acknowledging that the mosaic sarcophagus means the end of writing (and revising), and that the end of writing leads to an onslaught of potentially uncontrolled reading, James placed himself—really, his deified image and the text of his aesthetic covenant—at the gates to his literary world. In these texts—the eighteen New York Edition prefaces—James undergoes a metamorphosis, entering each one as the author-turned-reader and re-creating himself as the author of reading. John Carlos Rowe's reformulation of Roland Barthes's dictum "The birth of the reader must be at the cost of the death of the Author" applies here. Rowe writes, " 'The birth of reading occasions the death of the Author and the invention of the Reader,' in which an activity and problem of reading become the motivation for the fabrication of 'readers' and even of concepts of 'the reader.' "[15] Through the agency of the prefaces, James attempts to maintain his control over his fiction while sustaining its image of absolute formal integrity by reinventing himself as the model reader who leaves a track through the novels and tales that other, future readers— modernist readers—will follow. Taking the path of the author, the reader seems promised an ideal experience. Contrary to R. P. Blackmur's nominal contention that James intended the New York Edition prefaces as a guide to writers interested in "the art of the novel," the prefaces insinuate themselves as a guide to James's own readers.

In fact, the aesthetic of fiction that James articulates in each preface is personalized and highly individuated, complementing, perhaps relying on, the epistolary quality of the genre. In the prefaces, James places the novels and tales in the context of the author's articulated consciousness of his personal and professional history as well as in the context of his experience of reading (not to mention his extensive reading experience). That is, James

---

14. Foucault, "What is an Author?" 102–3.
15. Rowe, *Theoretical Dimensions*, 222.

refers repeatedly to his rereading of the works being prefaced, their place in his career, and his earlier reading of other literary works. The architecture of the Edition, on the other hand, is designed to transform the personal character of the author's experience of his work, which had insisted on dropping out, James said, into formal criticism that would on the one hand gesture toward the fiction's totality and, on the other, implicate the *reader's* need for supplementation. In this way, although he does not fully resolve the conflict of desires to be a powerful presence yet wholly ancillary to his fiction, James mitigates its most disturbing implication: that he has failed to create art with formal integrity.

1

What's in a Preface?
What's in a Frame?
What's in It for James?

> Tyger tyger burning bright,
> In the forests of the night;
> What immortal hand or eye,
> Could frame thy fearful symmetry?
> —William Blake

In the New York Edition prefaces, Henry James attempts to create the modern reader, one who is conscious of authorial performance and who judges it according to aesthetic principles rather than the social, political, or moral standards frequently applied to fiction during the previous century in England and America. To accomplish this feat, James developed several strategies to prepare the reader for the text. Thus to William Dean Howells James wrote that the prefaces were a "plea for appreciation." He added that they were also a plea for discrimination: he sought to repair and to recover the reader who had been educated in a different style of reading. James sought a select audience, and that audience, James knew at the turn of the century, would have to be created rather than wooed.

The reader envisioned in the prefaces receives the novels and tales of the New York Edition as both art and artifact, as "texts" in the sense that Roland Barthes means when he distinguishes *work* and *text:* "the work is a fragment of substance, occupying a part of the space of books (in a library for example), the Text is a methodological field"; the Text is "*radically* symbolic; *a work conceived, perceived and received in its integrally symbolic nature.*" The text focuses on the experience and nature of reading, as "play, activity, production, practice. This means," Barthes concludes, "that the Text requires that one try to abolish (or at the very least to diminish) the distance between writing and reading . . . by joining them in a single signifying practice."[1] The prefaces attempt to accomplish this diminution of distance by taking the work as the object of an idealized and authorized reading which they present; the reader is encouraged, sometimes manipulated, to adopt wholly the terms of James's writerly reading and transform the work into text by making it a methodological field. The prefaces describe James's method, in other words, and the prefaced narratives illustrate this method. In this way, reading becomes at least in part a didactic experience—an indoctrination. The prefaces demand that we ascribe aesthetic and, in the language of the marketplace, economic value to both the creation and the creator.

Although James adopts an epistolary tone in the prefaces, they never present themselves as supplemental texts offering interesting but largely insignificant gossip. They present themselves as privileged and empowered readings. They explicitly claim, for instance, that all that they contain is mined from the texts through the agency of authorial memory, which recalls while reading such things as the origin of the tale, the compositional problems and their solutions, the publication history, and critical reception. In other words, the prefaces gesture toward a cache of information and meaning that the narratives hoard. Yet only James, the author-turned-reader, can discover this store. No other reader is so privileged as he because no other reader has an eye on the writing's origins and methods of composition, which, John Carlos Rowe explains, are in the New York Edition "at least as important as the finished work itself, especially since the 'finish' of the work—its closure as well as its style—is nothing other than this very method objectified."[2] It becomes necessary, then, for James to provide the reader with that which the reader lacks, and this is the business of the prefaces.

The prefaces always look both inward and outward, repeatedly relating questions of composition and questions of reading. "The teller of a story is primarily, none the less, the listener to it, the reader of it, too," James asserts in the preface to *The Princess Casamassima* (5:viii). James as reader constantly defers to James as writer to enable the privileged reading that the prefaces provide. There's a poignant example of this in James's discussion of *The Spoils of Poynton*. The "old, shrunken concomitants" of writing and revising "lurk between the lines," which serve

---

1. Roland Barthes, "From Work to Text," *Image, Music, Text*, trans. Stephen Heath (New York: Hill and Wang, 1977), 156–57, 162.

2. Rowe, *Theoretical Dimensions of Henry James* (Madison: University of Wisconsin Press, 1984), 230.

as the barred seraglio-windows behind which, to the outsider in the glare of the Eastern street, forms indistinguishable seem to move and peer; "association" in fine bears upon them with its infinite magic. Peering through the lattice from without inward I recapture a cottage on a cliff-side, to which, as the earliest approach of the summer-time, redoubtable in London through the luxuriance of still other than "natural" forces, I had betaken myself to finish a book in quiet and to beginning another in fear. (10:x–xi)

James refers to the novel's sentences as impenetrable bars through which he as reader must peer in order to see what is truly inside this house of fiction. The image that he catches is not one of Fleda Vetch but of the cottage in which he wrote the novel. At this moment in the preface, James's novel is something that must be gone through, not entered into, if we are to arrive at this highly idiosyncratic but valuable reading. And the value of this reading is its discovery of the writer. We can not pass through the text, however, without James-the-reader as guide. Every morsel that he offers is a tantalizing reminder that he alone has access to the store of meaning latent in the text.

In this passage and many others, James is exploiting the public's desire for a glimpse into the private life of a public figure. James belonged to the first generation that saw the rise of book advertising and the cult of literary personality that issued from it. Indeed, James was something of a literary celebrity in America, as evidenced by the "constant comment" about his "expatriatism and slightly exotic philosophy of art," and by the "barrage of cartoons and commentary" about him during "his famous return journey to the United States in 1904–5."[3] Yet James's works were not especially marketable, and so he decided to use the Edition prefaces to attract readers familiar with the celebrity and anxious for information about him, and to make use of his status to capture the reader long enough to indoctrinate him or her into his aesthetic of fiction. Borus reveals James's logic when he explains that the celebrity status accorded to famous authors in James's era made the "activity [of authoring] itself . . . more fascinating than the results" to the reading public, and that therefore the novel was superseded "as the meeting place between writer and reader" by advertisements and other media that spoke of "both the book and its creator" (128). In essence,

---

3. Daniel H. Borus, *Writing Realism: Howells, James, and Norris in the Mass Market* (Chapel Hill: University of North Carolina Press, 1989), 126.

if the readers would not come to his novels and tales, James would meet them where he could find them—in works about the novels, tales, and the author himself—in the frame. Michael Anesko claimed recently, in fact, that "James's famous prefaces might be read as a rather copious advertisement for the edition."[4] Apparently, James decided that author and reader would meet on his own ground—the prefaces—and he began working assiduously to survey that ground and claim it.

James embarks on his mission to attract celebrity-conscious readers by declaring in the first preface that the prefaces are concerned with both author and artwork: "These notes represent over a considerable course, the continuity of an artist's endeavour, the growth of his whole operative consciousness and, best of all, perhaps, their own tendency to multiply, with the implication, thereby, of a memory much enriched" (1:vi). Calling the prefaces *notes*, James reminds us that he is providing what he calls "the *accessory* facts in a given artistic case" from a source—a notebook, his memory—that is, antecedent to the finished work and to which only he has access (1:vi). Yet the context allows sufficient ambiguity for us to read "notes" as a reference to the epistolary nature of the prefaces: they are notes to his reader, as if in recognition that the prefaces are the meeting place between writer and reader of which Borus speaks.

By guiding the reader through his own revisionary, self-referential tour during which he, in the guise of "the painter who passes over his old sunk canvas a wet sponge that shows him what may still come out again," James teases the reader with a promise "that the canvas *has* kept a few buried secrets" not yet revealed (1:xiii). Reading the preface narrative of James's work as author, in other words, will result in a reading of the prefaced text that is more richly suggestive and far more rewarding for inquiring minds than a reading of that novel or tale without such preparation. And this holds true, James says, for the "present array of earlier, later, larger, smaller" works of the entire Edition.

The first secret revealed after this promise of hidden delights is not some personal confession, not even a subtlety of character or artistry, but a flaw that "just fails to wreck" the novel: the "time-scheme of the story is quite inadequate," James announces. "Everything occurs . . . too punctually and moves too fast: Roderick's disintegration, a gradual process, and of which the

---

4. Michael Anesko, "Review of Ann T. Margolis, *Henry James and the Problem of Audience: An Intentional Act* and Jennifer A. Wicke, *Advertising Fictions: Literature, Advertisement, and Social Reading,*" *Henry James Review* 12 (1991): 85.

exhibitional interest is exactly that it *is* gradual and occasional, and thereby traceable and watchable, swallows two years in a mouthful, proceeds quite *not* by years, but by weeks and months, and thus renders the whole view the disservice of appearing to present him as a morbidly special case" (1:xiv). Such criticism certainly might have been leveled against the novel by any of James's critics, but it is presented here as the first buried secret revealed by the author's revelatory application of varnish. The strategy that James seems to be employing is to make critical evaluation of his work the responsibility of the privileged reader, the one who has the authority to take the reins of authorship and revise the work and thereby to protect the work (as art and as commodity) from the untutored and too often disparaging reader. James is accepting responsibility for the text, perfect or flawed, and this is the first prerequisite to assumption of authority over one's work according to J. Hillis Miller.[5] James's strategy is bound to disappoint the reader of celebrity biography, and indeed Howells expressed his wish that the prefaces were far more biographical and less concerned with James's fiction.

The prefaces are the only semiotic realm where James's motives could unite in a single discourse that would at least attempt to fulfill his desires. They exist in the space of mediation between the literary and extraliterary worlds; they occupy the space of the windows of the house of fiction, to use James's elegant metaphor. Only from this space can James attempt to control reading of his work without entering that work as an interloper who would invalidate the aesthetic he seeks to promote. Only at the semiotic border of his novels and tales can James make himself felt as both presence and absence. At the semiotic border, participating in the discourses of both the literary and extraliterary realms that they separate, however, the prefaces seem to belie the reality of a definitive border. Moreover, they render problematic the relation of frame and framed narrative that informs the Edition's architecture, as dialogue among recent frame theorists suggests. John Frow contends that "the frame of course is unitary, neither inside nor outside, and this distinction of levels must be seen as a convenient fiction to express the frame's dual status as a component of structure and a component of situation. For a literary text, it works both as an enclosure of the internal fictional space and as an exclusion of the space of reality against which the work is set; but this operation of exclusion is also an inclusion of the

5. See J. Hillis Miller, *The Ethics of Reading: Kant, de Man, Eliot, Trollope, James, and Benjamin* (New York: Columbia University Press, 1987), 106–7.

text in this alien space."[6] Frow reminds us of the frame's role as mediator, but unlike Boris Uspensky, who argues that the frame is an extraliterary event that indicates to the reader that the semiotic field is near at hand, Frow does not consider the frame as an element of either artistic or extra-artistic space.[7] Barbara Johnson, in contrast, notes that there are compelling contradictions in framing that cannot be resolved so easily. She claims that "the total inclusion of the 'frame' is both mandatory and impossible. The 'frame' thus becomes not the borderline between the inside and outside, but precisely what subverts the applicability of the inside/outside polarity to the act of interpretation."[8] All literary and pictorial frames not only differentiate realms and identify that which they enclose, but, according to John Matthews, they also exist "as a function which enables a relation between differentiated realms (the reader and author, the world and the artwork, reality and imagination, and so on)."[9] Clearly, it is this *relation*, not the reader or the texts themselves, that James longs to control.

In this light, one might argue that the prefaces do not serve their primary function when divorced from the fictive texts to which they were written in response. Yet the definitive edition of the prefaces is generally considered to be R. P. Blackmur's edition of them, boldly titled *The Art of the Novel.*[10] The title suggests a view of the prefaces as definitive and independent texts that has been so pervasive that it is worthwhile to consider it at some length here before arguing for the semiotic integrity of the prefaces and the narrative worlds they articulate as well as for the integrity of the Edition as a whole. Blackmur believes that James wrote the prefaces to instruct would-be novelists and to provide his readers with the ideal critical discourse for application to the Jamesian text, the lack of which discourse was the primary cause for James's relative failure at the literary marketplace. "Criticism has never been more ambitious, nor more useful," Blackmur writes in his introduction. "There has never been a body of work so eminently suited to criticism as the fiction of Henry James, and there has certainly never been

6. John Frow, "The Literary Frame," *Journal of Aesthetic Education* 16, no. 2 (1982): 29.

7. Boris Uspensky, *A Poetics of Composition*, trans. Valentina Zavarin and Susan Wittig (Berkeley and Los Angeles: University of California Press, 1973).

8. Barbara Johnson, "The Frame of Reference: Poe, Lacan, Derrida," *Yale French Studies* 55–56 (1977): 481.

9. John T. Matthews, "Framing in *Wuthering Heights*," *Texas Studies in Literature and Language* 27 (Spring 1985): 26.

10. *The Art of the Novel: Critical Prefaces by Henry James*, with an Introduction by Richard P. Blackmur (New York: Charles Scribner's Sons, 1934).

an author who saw the need and had the ability to criticise specifically and at length his own work." And as Hershel Parker argues, "the best critics of James, whether following Blackmur or, less often, like Holland and Jefferson, modifying Blackmur's reading of the prefaces, have continued to treat *The Art of the Novel* as a regular book by Henry James," one that has "tyrannized" over James's readers.[11] Blackmur's edition severs the prefaces from the narratives they precede, believing that the prefaces have "a being aside from any connection with [James's] own work, and that finally, they [add] up to a fairly exhaustive reference book on the technical aspects"—not, Blackmur says, of James's fiction, and not of James's literary aesthetic, but "of the art of fiction" unqualified.[12] Blackmur's enthusiasm and, perhaps, his accurate assessment of the reach of James's ambition, ultimately apply the prefaces to the entire genre rather than to the texts for which they were specifically written. Blackmur responds strongly to James's desire for control by becoming perhaps James's most finely indoctrinated reader. *The Art of the Novel* seeks to further James's goal of supplementing readers of his fiction by extending the terms of his discourse onto readers of other works, and onto other authors as well.

Comparing the prefaces to Aristotle's *Poetics*, Blackmur makes the formalist moves of first severing the prefaces from the novels and tales they introduce, and then removing them from the individual, historical, and literary contexts in which they were written. Yet personal, literary, and even economic history flood the prefaces, as Blackmur's introductory categorization of theme implies.[13] Collecting the prefaces as a "fairly exhaustive reference book," as Blackmur has done, alters the work and nature of the prefaces by attempting to convert them into chapters; in *The Art of the Novel*, the prefaces displace the prefaced novels and tales, the parasitic supplement having devoured its host. The prefaces are, of course, some of James's finest critical writing; they are, however, *excerpts* from a much longer work—the New York Edition.

The Edition is a federation of texts—prefaces, novels, tales—in which each novel and tale is independent, has borders that make it discrete from

11. Hershel Parker, "Deconstructing *The Art of the Novel* and Liberating James's Prefaces," *Henry James Review* 14 (1993): 287, 285.

12. Blackmur, introduction to *The Art of the Novel*, xv, xvi.

13. Quentin Anderson is perhaps the first to call for consideration of the historical and cultural influences on James's life and work. See *The Imperial Self: An Essay in American Literary and Cultural History* (New York: Knopf, 1971), esp. 166–244.

all neighboring texts, and is governed by its own internal logic. In some instances, groups of stories are joined in one volume and enleagued by a single preface, and several of the novels require two volumes. Ultimately, however, all the novels and tales participate in the New York Edition as narrative exempla within the author's critical discourse of the prefaces, at the end of each of which the author temporarily disappears and is replaced by the fictive world that is reflected in the subjective consciousness constructed in the novel or tale. The prefaces are stripped of their transformative power, therefore, when they are shorn from the texts that they were created to transform. They are critical discourse that relates two realms—the literary and the extraliterary—yet in Blackmur's presentation of them, the literary realm has been amputated and the extraliterary is suppressed.

The New York Edition prefaces are conceptually similar to the traditional literary frame that enleagues several narratives by providing a situational context for the act of narration. In the *Arabian Nights*, for example, Scheherazade narrates from the frame, in which each tale prolongs her life for another day; and Chaucer's pilgrims make their way toward Canterbury as if propelled by the telling of tales. In *The Castle of Crossed Destinies*, Italo Calvino's mute dealers of the tarot deck use the visual cues of the cards to recite their life histories. Their narrations are a means of freeing themselves from the yoked curses of forced silence and the compulsion to articulate the past. All tell stories from the frame. The speakers exist corporeally outside the tales they tell and are the immediate verbal origins of those tales. The tales are objects that signify in a discourse outside themselves. In each case, *outside* the tale is *inside* the frame.

The tales exist *as tales* in the narrative of the frame and thereby enhance the illusion that the frame narrative represents a real world; the tale exists as an event within the constraints of the frame's narratological time, but framing deprives the tales themselves of such an illusion. In fact, Scheherazade's tales are metonymic transformations of narratological time: each tale substitutes for the passage of one night. In this instance, the framed narrative gives substance and physical extension to the frame: without the embedded tales, all the Arabian nights would pass as quickly and in the same textual space as any one or more of them.

The force with which the frame makes its presence felt varies, and its effect on the framed tales varies proportionally. The distinction between the frames of *The Canterbury Tales* and the *Decameron* suggests the differences between viable, complex, engaging frame narratives that have the potential of subsuming the framed tales, and thin, flat, relatively uninteresting frame narratives that offer little more than an excuse for presenting the framed tales. The frame, as a supplement, is what Derrida defines as "that which is not internal or intrinsic . . . , as an integral part . . . , to the total representation of the object . . . but which belongs to it only in an extrinsic way . . . as a surplus, an addition, an adjunct."[14] As supplement, the frame to the *Decameron* or to *The Canterbury Tales*, for example, implies that the tales are lacking; yet the frame is also lacking: it requires the tales to inflate it into appreciable existence. The tales could not exist *as tales* without the frame to provide the context in which narration occurs; the frame would be empty without the tales, constantly gesturing toward nothing. The frame and the framed tales collude to mask the inadequacy of each constituent to stand on its own. Yet a frame narrative may be so rich and compelling, as the prefaces apparently are to Blackmur and others, that it becomes liberated from its subordinate context and threatens to subsume the tales it supplements. The embedded tales would then become subordinate to the embedding narrative, as is the case in Philip Roth's *Ghost Writer*, for example, in which a brief dream sequence is embedded in an overwhelming frame narrative of a young man's visit to an older writer's home.[15] Or the framed narratives will simply cease to exist, as is the case in *The Art of the Novel.*

Like the traditional multiple-narrative literary frame, the prefaces to the New York Edition provide context and relation. In these prefaces, however, both functions are formal, aesthetic, thematic, and sometimes narratological. The prefaces do not differ significantly from traditional narrative frames in that they present a narrative situation in which the tales are being read (by the author-turned-reader in the act of revision), and they place the novels and tales in the ongoing narrative context of James's revision and preparation of the New York Edition. Yet the linking of the novels and tales is made problematic by this context. Rather than presenting a framed

14. Derrida, *The Truth in Painting*, trans. Geoff Bennington and Ian McLeod (Chicago: University of Chicago Press, 1987), 57.

15. In this case, the frame becomes what Jacques Derrida calls a *parergon*. Literally, the "around work," the *parergon*, writes Derrida, "is not simply [an] exteriority as a surplus, it is the internal structural link which rivets [it] to the lack in the interior of the *ergon* [the work]. And this lack would be constitutive of the very unity of the *ergon*. Without this lack, the *ergon* would have no need of a *parergon*." A type of supplement, the *parergon* is both ancillary and necessary to the center around which it exists. What distinguishes the *parergon* from other supplements is its function as that which *constitutes* "the very unity of the *ergon*": it delineates the work both spatially and temporally and therefore allows the *ergon* to exist as such. Thus the framed narrative becomes meaningful only as it is framed. Without the frame, the framed narrative *as it is* would be effectively destroyed. *Truth in Painting*, 59–60.

tale as either a response to a previously told tale or as a means of bringing about a hoped-for result within the plot in the frame narrative, for instance, the contextualizing function of James's prefaces situates the tales in the process of the author's creation and consumption of his work. The tales are related by contingency and contiguity rather than causality. Consequently, this Edition's semiotic integrity depends on a precarious spatial order: the frame is anterior to its framed content, but the framed narratives do not directly respond to one another within a frame narrative nor do they depend upon the frame for substance or context. In this respect, James's prefaces have an analogue in the plastic arts. The panels of a triptych participate in a complex semiotic field that extends across the three panels. Each panel is understood in relation to the concept that joins them together. The triptych is perceived as a compound semiotic unit because the panels are physically conjoined or juxtaposed through the agency of the frame. Each panel could be understood individually, with no broader semiotic field determining meaning, just as any one of James's novels might be read independently of his other works, but the physical bond achieved by the frame prevents such an isolating gesture and encourages an intertextual reading that depends upon a conceptual frame of reference that does not exist in any one panel or in the frame itself, but as a consequence of the entire semiotic structure.

This model of framing offered by the plastic arts is static. The panels of a triptych are joined by a rigid, usually hinged frame, the physical function of which is to assure unity, spatial arrangement, and differentiation of the pictures or panels. The artist usually relies on traditional relationships of ideas (the stages of man, the Trinity, and so forth) that the artist can assume are understood by the work's spectators, to provide and convey the conceptual frame that interrelates the paintings as a group or series. In lieu of a critical introduction, the physical frame implies a conceptual frame of reference, indicating how one should "read" the paintings and how one should understand them in relation to one another. The frame is bankrupt of meaning without the framed panels. Similarly, the New York Edition prefaces create unity, arrangement, and differentiation. They articulate the conceptual framework of the Edition as a whole and of its individual volumes, and they indicate how the framed narratives should be read. They are clearly different than the multipanel frame because they are themselves texts.

As texts, prefaces are meant to precede other texts on which they are contingent. A preface "pre-makes" (*pre facio*), describing the principal action (or describing around the principal action) before the action takes place.

This of course is the order in which the preface and prefaced text are experienced by the reader. The historical view is that James wrote the prefaces after he wrote and revised the novels and tales. Thus the Edition prefaces are situated before, but refer back to, the narratives as they have been read by the author. Prior to reading a novel, in other words, James's reader experiences that novel as a text already read; moreover, the reader experiences this already-read text indirectly, as the author's experience of having read—an experience that recalls and recovers the author's even more antecedent act of having written the text.[16]

Gayatri Chakravorty Spivak argues in her "Translator's Preface" to Jacques Derrida's *Of Grammatology* that all prefaces are written a posteriori and affixed to appear a priori. She postulates that reading is a circular event, not a linear one, and concludes that the placement of the preface in relation to the prefaced text is less relevant than one might assume. That is, a preface might just as well be experienced by the reader as it is by the writer, as a postface. And of course many readers choose to read the preface (or to return to it) after they have finished with the novel. Thus for James's reader, the preface either prereads or rereads the narrative; it either prepares the reader or repairs him. Because James's prefaces locate the narratives of the New York Edition in the author's critical consciousness as his creation and as an object of his own readerly consumption, each Edition preface presents the narrative as an event of authorial consciousness and as an act of authorized reading meant to be duplicated, whether the preface is read before or after the narrative. And because the track that James's reading leaves through the narratives uncovers meaning where any reader other than James would find nothing more than absence, the prefaces permanently alter the prefaced novels and tales by expanding them through the agency of the privileged author's delegate: the educated (that is to say, the "prefaced") reader. For instance, of *The Tragic Muse*, James writes, "it contains nothing better . . . than that preserved and achieved unity and quality of tone." "The appeal," James continues, "the fidelity to the prime motive, is, with no little art, strained clear (even as silver is polished) in a degree answering—at least by intention—to the air of beauty" (7:xxii). The prime motive to which *The*

---

16. Julie Rivkin argues along similar lines: "written after the novel and printed before it, following the novel's composition and yet providing an account of origins, supposedly extrinsic to the text and yet based on it," the prefaces offer an "account of origins . . . [that] can be derived from the novels themselves." "The Logic of Delegation in *The Ambassadors*," *PMLA* 101 (1986): 821.

Tragic Muse remains faithful—to present "the conflict between art and 'the world' "—is articulated only in the preface; only by reading the preface, then, could James's reader fully appreciate the novel in the manner, and to the degree, that James desires (though certainly some readers might come to that text already indoctrinated, already prepared to discriminate and appreciate James's work of art without reading the preface).

The copious relations between preface and prefaced narrative construct a dialogic discourse that defines the preface (at the semiotic border) and the narrative (as the primary semiotic field) as responses to one another that rely upon a constant play or exchange of self and other, of writer and reader. The preface presents, in Felman's words, "a reading of the other, . . . [the preface] is a story in the other, a story whose signification is interfered with but whose interference is significant, a story whose meaning interferes but whose interference means."[17] The framed narrative has been infiltrated by the story of its own creation, for example, that the author uncovers through his reading of the text. Thus the story in the preface is a story that exists but is suppressed in the narrative. Conversely, the narrative interferes in the preface because it is located there as the author's reading of a text that has not yet been encountered by the preface reader. The preface temporarily delays the narrative, but it eventually yields to the reader's desire for the narrative that it has incited after it has successfully created an authorized reading—what John Carlos Rowe refers to more generally as an author-reader function.

"The *problem* of the textual situation," John Carlos Rowe writes, "provokes the need for an author-reader function, for the determination of a certain set of relations that might provide a frame or boundary for the 'text.' "[18] Indeed, the "certain set of relations" is provided in the frame that the textual situation necessitates. The frame "is meant to change one's conception of its interior space," first by defining interiority (and, by implicit contrast, exteriority), and then by deconstructing the opposition.[19] The frame is a vortex, drawing in both the extraliterary world of the reader, the marginal world of the author, and the fictive world it defines. Thus it ultimately negates itself as the dividing line and is replaced by the relationship—the contract, really—between author and reader that it (re)constitutes.

17. Shoshana Felman, "Turning the Screw of Interpretation," *Yale French Studies* 55–56 (1977): 125.

18. Rowe, *Theoretical Dimensions*, 223.

19. Germano Celant, "Framed: Innocence or Gilt?" *Artforum* 20 (Summer 1980): 51.

Recently critics have begun to recover the extraliterary influences that Blackmur and others ignored. William Goetz and Mutlu Blasing argue in quite different contexts that the prefaces are essentially autobiographical; Vivien Jones and David Seed have written of the construction of the author in the prefaces. Yet most critics stubbornly retain the traditional view that the prefaces are privileged criticism, above textual and most especially contextual analyses. They implicitly agree that the prefaces have unique authority over the prefaced narratives, asserting as Morris Robert does, that the prefaces are "the best possible commentaries on [James's] own work," yet they overlook the implications of the simple fact that the prefaces are James's own work; they are the writing of James's desire for eternal appreciation and discrimination—for reverence. Those who have questioned the prevailing assumptions about the prefaces generally do so marginally. Shoshana Felman, for example, calls the preface to *The Turn of the Screw*, "a prologue to the prologue, an introduction to the introduction," and thereby invites questions of doubling and repetition. Laurence Holland begins his lengthy discussion of *The Portrait of a Lady* with a critical analysis of its preface, implying but never stating that the preface is part of the aesthetic structure under critical scrutiny. And Julie Rivkin frames her discussion of the logic of delegation in *The Ambassadors* with a meticulous recovery of the logic of delegation in the preface to that novel.[20]

James was conscious of the relation between frame and framed texts. Near the end of the preface to *The Wings of the Dove* he admits, "I become conscious of overstepping my space" (19:xxv). He silences himself, when, on the edge of the frame and facing the prefaced narrative, he fears that he has not "brought the full quantity" of his reading "to light" but realizes that his reading is overpowered by the reader's desire for the framed text. He recognizes his marginal position and utterly fears compromising the narrative by remaining visible in the composition as either creator or consumer; however, James wants to remain in a central and imperial relation to his work of art, and so he must, finally, deconstruct the author-reader polarity as well. Only through the act of reading can the complex aesthetic structure that

---

20. See Vivien Jones, *James the Critic* (New York: St. Martin's, 1985); David Seed, "The Narrator in Henry James's Criticism," *Philological Quarterly* 60 (1981): 501–21; Morris Robert, *Henry James's Criticism* (New York: Octagon Books, 1970), 83; Shoshana Felman, "Turning the Screw of Interpretation," 122; Laurence Holland, *Expense of Vision: Essays on the Craft of Henry James* (Princeton: Princeton University Press, 1964); Julie Rivkin, "The Logic of Delegation in *The Ambassadors*."

includes author and work, preface and narrative, composition and frame, be created. For the aesthetic structure that is expansive enough to be so inclusive is ultimately a construction in (and of) the reader's consciousness. As James disappears behind the fictive text for the last time in the Edition, he admits that he cannot fully enclose and control his narratives within hermetic frames of reference. However, as creator his "relation to them is essentially traceable," by the thoroughly colonized reader; "and in that fact abides," James admits, "incomparable luxury" (23:xxv).

2

THE POLITICS
OF THE
PREFACE

In the preface to *The Golden Bowl*, James contends that "the frame of one's own work no more provides place for" an illustrator's vision or other extraliterary forms of supplementation, "than we expect flesh and fish to be served on the same platter" (23:x). James's culinary orthodoxy aside, his assertion that the frame—the semiotic border—is the sole property of the author, and his use of the frame to protect his artwork from intruding and competing discourses, are thoroughly informed by late nineteenth-century practices and politics of framing. More generally, the strategies that James employs in the prefaces as he attempts to create the ideal reader of his work have a long history of analogues and antecedents in literary practice and in the plastic arts. This history helps explain why James sought to make the prefaces a complex "plea for appreciation and discrimination," as he told Howells they must be.

The preface is traditionally the site in which the rights of authorship are claimed and the power to authorize the text is assumed. Prefatory assertions of authority seem almost endemic to the novel in particular, owing perhaps to its fairly recent emergence as a distinct genre and the lack, therefore, of basic a priori assumptions about how that genre works. For example, as Michael McKeon describes it, Cervantes found his authority and his authorial identity threatened almost immediately after Part 1 of *Don Quixote* was published. Alonso Fernández de Avellaneda wrote a sequel, claiming that it was the "true" continuation of his work. Cervantes responded by writing a preface to his own Part 2, in which he claims authenticity for his sequel. His Part 2, Cervantes implicitly argues, is authentic because it was written by the same man who authored Part 1. The preface to Part 2, in other words, makes a claim of value for the novel based on the value of its author as determined by his previous literary performance. The preface also constructs a relationship between text and world that might otherwise not exist: Cervantes brings his own characters into the ambiguous space of the frame to speak for him and his work. McKeon explains that, "Cervantes is able to forbear from 'revengeful Invectives' against Avellaneda in his second 'Preface' because he knows that definitive distinctions between true and false histories"—that is, between Cervantes's Part 2 and Avellaneda's—"will be insisted upon by some of his characters."[1] Voices from the fictive world speak in the frame, and later, in the fiction, the claims of authenticity made in the frame are supported. Preface and novel collaborate rather than conflict; and as a result, the two texts unite as a compound semiotic structure that signifies the individual powers and rights of authorship.

Cervantes's second preface both mediates between and enleagues the real world and the world of the novel. It acknowledges and addresses what Ian Watt calls the central problem of the modern novel's origins in early eighteenth-century realism: "the problem of the correspondence between the literary work and the reality which it imitates."[2] Watt argues in the first chapter of *The Rise of the Novel* that novelists such as Richardson and Fielding struggled within their novels to be true to individual experience. They also attempted to construct a relation between their work and the world of the reader. The structure of Watt's argument gestures toward the novels' two lives as work and text, to recall Barthes's distinction, which informs many prefaces from those of Cervantes to James and beyond. The novel is both object and experience; it is owned and read. It therefore registers in two value systems, the economic and the aesthetic. Cervantes's preface to Part 2 of *Don Quixote*, like James's prefaces to the New York Edition, directly confronts the novel's problematic existence as a mimetically "real" world framed by and therefore confined within the real world of the reader which it

1. Michael McKeon, *The Origins of the English Novel* (Baltimore: Johns Hopkins University Press, 1987), 275.

2. Ian Watt, *The Rise of the Novel: Studies in Defoe, Richardson and Fielding* (Berkeley and Los Angeles: University of California Press, 1957), 11.

imitates, and as a real object in the reader's world. This confrontation leaves the semiotic border, which is occupied by the preface, an intensely volatile field that extends across the generally recognized borders that separate these worlds. Cervantes's preface demarks the literary semiotic field from within that field and from outside it (unlike, for example, an introduction by an esteemed reader, which represents consumption rather than origin of the text). Cervantes's preface bespeaks a desire for validation of, and authority over, the text. As McKeon implies, authorship is defined in this frame as both an aesthetic and an economic title, the rights and privileges accompanying which depend on both the prevailing conceptions of the relation of art and the world, and the relation of authority and boundary—of power and property.

One of the primary tasks of the New York Edition prefaces is to draw a defensible boundary around James's works and thereby to protect his aesthetic of fiction, which is to say, his literary career. The prefaces seem repeatedly to stave off attacks, citing as opponents such figures as literary historians who would take possession of James and his works as historical artifacts that signify in the historians' narratives; critics who second-guess James and devalue his aesthetic choices; arbiters of literary economics, who did not find James's work marketable; and the untutored reader who, like some clumsy tourist, would trample through the texts. To this end, James casts himself as both defender and exemplary reader of the text (which, he hopes, will show the way to consumers of the work). In the preface to *The Golden Bowl*, which as the final preface is James's last and most dramatic stand in defense of the semiotic border, James diplomatically insinuates himself in the path of the approaching historian: "As the historian of the matter sees and speaks, so my intelligence of it, as a reader, meets him halfway, passive, receptive, appreciative, often even grateful; unconscious, quite blissfully, of any bar to intercourse, any disparity of sense between us. Into his very footprints the responsive, the imaginative steps of the docile reader that I consentingly become for him all comfortably sink" (23:xiii). James wants to determine, in other words, how his works will be read by literary history by first encountering and then becoming the literary historian. In this instance, he dares not reject literary history for he is consciously creating it. Instead, James becomes a willing, apparently (and deceptively) docile collaborator who seeks control over historical narrative by contributing to it. We shall return later in this chapter to James's defensiveness, particularly as it manifests itself in his discussion of the Coburn photographs that both collaborate with James to control reading and question his authority by offering another reader's vision. The historical context of James's use of the semiotic border as a means of empowerment and control should be established first in order to clarify James's motives and methods.

Assertion of authority at the semiotic border has been neither a consistent nor widely recognized convention. Giving voice to this space which is neither inside nor outside is fraught with ambivalence and contradiction. The epic poet's invocation of the muses, for example, frames the epic with a direct address by the poet that paradoxically asserts the poet's presence and denies his authorial power. The epic poet relegates the authority of creation to the muses, thus making himself a conduit connecting the transcendent realm of Art and the earthly realm of representation. *The Canterbury Tales* is framed by the story of the pilgrimage, which defines the tales as fictions that have meaning within the framing story. Chaucer effectively denies the powers of creation by narrating through a substitute and by attributing the tales to speakers who take on the illusion of reality through the agency of the frame. Exposing the ambivalence of such authorial self-suppression, Nabokov begins *Lolita* with a foreword by John Ray, Jr., Ph.D., who attests to Humbert Humbert's historicity, and ends with an artful unmasking of his authority: the afterword begins, "After doing my impersonation of suave John Ray, the character in Lolita who pens the Foreword, my comments coming straight from me may strike one—may strike me, in fact—as an impersonation of Vladimir Nabokov talking about his own book" (282). Nabokov initially forsakes authorship, then he champions his rights to authority over the text, its subject matter, and its aesthetic of fiction to respond, at least ostensibly, to its harshest critics. In the course of it all, he suggests that authorship is itself a mask: tracing original authority, the reader finds him- or herself in a hall of mirrors that continue to reflect an originating object no longer present. James was acutely aware of this and sought in the prefaces to affix a representation of authorial consciousness to his works of fiction, hoping in that way to unmask himself as author and to assert authority over the text by becoming both its creator and model reader. He positions himself at the semiotic border because this is where the realm of the author gives way to the realm of the reader.

The rise of realism and the simultaneous commodification of art that Ian Watt describes affected the visual arts in much the same way and in the same place as they affected the novel: the semiotic field and its border became volatile and politicized. Art historians, like Meyer Schapiro and Germano Celant, recognize a transformation of the picture frame in

France, Britain, and America during the nineteenth century.[3] They argue that frames changed as conceptions of the framed compositions changed in response to the rise of realism in Europe and later in America. By the end of the century, many frames around paintings and those preceding (sometimes infiltrating) stories were produced as experiments by painters and writers who annexed the borders of literary and visual semiotic fields and used these boundaries to control the relation of the artwork and the world of the reader.

A brief history of the frame's relation to the semiotic field supports this contention. Schapiro points out that prehistoric cave drawings were frequently superimposed over other drawings, as if the drawings were a temporary expression, like a message written on a chalkboard. With no physical or lasting temporal borders and with no implication of background extension, each cave drawing has a sense of immediacy and presence as if the subject were somehow part of the spectator's, not the aesthetic, realm of existence. Apparently, the drawing had no individual (really, both economic and aesthetic) value to the artist or spectator apart from its role as sign. To prehistoric artists, the shared locus of expression was more significant over the course of time than the expression itself. Thus the location of their semiotic field was relatively constant, while its content was continually being compounded or erased. Discovered and authenticated in the last decade of the nineteenth century, these cave drawings became "the seminal force in modern art history" according to Hugh Kenner.[4]

The semiotic field was not privileged until art was used to cover or disguise utilitarian objects. Schapiro traces the history of the "continuous isolating frame around an image," which he aptly characterizes as "a homogeneous enclosure like a city wall," to late in the second millennium B.C., when framing appears as a common practice in Greek art, particularly as part of the decoration of urns and vases.[5] Pictorial compositions were imposed upon objects of lasting value and, like those objects, were granted distinct physical boundaries. The frame, often a thin line at the composition's margin, created an aesthetic, semiotic field by demarking its boundaries,

3. Celant, "Framed: Innocence or Gilt?" *Artforum* 20 (Summer 1980): 49–55; Meyer Schapiro, "On Some Visual Problems in the Semiotics of Visual Art: Field and Vehicle in Image-Signs," *Semiotica* 1, no. 3 (1969): 223–42.

4. Hugh Kenner, *The Pound Era* (Berkeley and Los Angeles: University of California Press, 1971), 29.

5. Schapiro, "On Some Visual Problems," 226–27.

thus separating this field from the world it represents and, most particularly, distinguishing it from the utilitarian aspect of its background. As Jeffrey Hurwit explains, these boundaries distinguish the borders of the visual semiotic field from the edges and contours of the object on which it is painted.[6]

By the seventeenth century, the frame, usually burnished gold (the color of value), had become heavy and ornate. The intricate design of this frame was seldom consonant with the picture; if it was, the harmony was co-incidental. Nevertheless, these overwhelming structures bordered nearly every painting in museums and in most bourgeois and aristocratic homes in Europe and America for more than two hundred years. The common practice of placing fairly inexpensive copies of famous paintings in gilt frames reveals the purpose of such a frame: the frame as a sign of value enhances the worth of the copy by lending it meaning in the semiotics of economy. This frame is able to help orient the spectator because it belongs to the spectator's extra-artistic realm. The frame's purpose, in this case, is to announce the closed, tectonic border that is presumed to exist between the conceptual realm of art, which it contains, and the world, in which it suggests the function of art as commodity. Therefore, these frames demark, as do all property lines (and city walls), a recognizable, verifiable border that is presumably drawn according to some logic inherent in the difference between art and the world—a difference that without the frame, would still somehow conceptually distinguish the two realms (though it would not ensure the freedom of either realm from intrusion of the other).

By the 1850s, British, French, and American artists had begun to reclaim the borders of their paintings as rightfully part of the aesthetic property of the composition. French Realist Gustave Courbet, for example, framed one landscape with freshly cut pine boughs. He wanted to create in the frame space an organic response to the subject on the canvas. Pine boughs com-plement the scene painted rather than contradict the scene's naturalness, as would a gilt rococo frame. He rebelled against the ideology of the traditional, ornate golden frame, which announces resoundingly that the painting is a materially revered object to be set like a gem; such a frame clearly signifies the status of ownership. This frame in particular locates the authority of ownership in the discursive realm from which it takes its meaning—outside

6. Jeffrey Hurwitt, "Image and Frame in Greek Art," *American Journal of Archaeology* 18, no. 1 (1977): 1–30.

the painting—and so disempowers the artist even though he or she is the author of aesthetic vision.

The gradual reconception of the frame as an element of the composition, rather than as an element of the extra-artistic space, implied a transfer of authority from consumer to artist. While these artists were reacting to economic exploitation, Realist writers and painters of James's generation and immediately preceding him were reinscribing the path of exploitation by demanding control over the consumption of their aesthetic goods by creating an educated public that would desire these artworks because they had been taught to appreciate them, much as colonies are politically and psychologically captive markets for the culture and goods of the ruling nation.

By the late nineteenth century both art and power in the Western world were characterized by the dissemination of European and British culture and by the extension of its economic dominions. Political boundaries described the spheres of ethnographic and economic influence. In a sense, then, political boundaries serve as semiotic borders: they establish a physical space wherein a determined set of laws govern. Late nineteenth-century artists' concerns with degrees of aesthetic and economic authority engaged in the politics of boundary-making: their frames, at the boundaries of art, established what might be called aesthetic empires. These artists were responding to a number of factors, including the limitations of national and especially international copyright laws (before 1891) that virtually endorsed pirating of manuscripts to the economic detriment of writers and publishers alike, and the Realists' philosophical and aesthetic negation of the Romantic belief that both creation and consumption of art are purely subjective experiences (that art, in fact, reflects subjectivity).

The early French Impressionist painters, whose work strongly influenced James's transformation of realism, first abandoned the traditional gilt frame, claiming the frame space as part of the composition.[7] Edgar Degas, for example, substituted a narrow, plain white-painted wooden border (resembling the margins of a printed page) that he believed neither added to nor detracted from the aesthetic of the composition. Degas's frames were meant to be neutral. He attempted to suppress the proprietary discourse of the traditional frame by denying the border itself; as a result, the framing space

---

7. On James and literary impressionism, see H. Peter Stowell, *Literary Impressionism: James and Chekhov* (Athens: University of Georgia Press, 1980).

became an unstable environ allowing him to experiment with alternative modes of aesthetic enclosure. For example, his objectivity toward nature led to experiments with photographs and monotypes that, framed as aesthetic compositions, attempt to disorient the spectator by obscuring the distinction between the world within the frame and the world without.

In his canvases, Degas questioned the borders of the artwork by creating the illusion that the pictorial composition extends beyond the canvas rather than "ends" before it encounters the frame. Figures at the edge are often only half seen, as if they exist in some pictorial space beyond the edge of the canvas, thereby suggesting that a painting is only one section of an aesthetic plane whose extension is indeterminate if not infinite. Thus the frame served for Degas as a cover over what Celant calls the slit or wound where the aesthetic plane emerges from beneath the real, exterior world— or where reality rises all around and covers art.[8] Degas's technique denies the frame as a marker of the periphery of the aesthetic plane; by suggesting that the pictorial has indeterminate or infinite extension beyond the spectator's range of vision, it calls attention to the power of the artist to delineate a particular composition by tracing its semiotic border. The technique imbues the act of framing with a power to control aesthetic space that is directly linked to the authority of the individual artistic consciousness.

Approximately twenty years after Degas's first experiments, Georges Seurat found in the framing space that separates his pointillist paintings from the world they inhabit a location for a painterly discourse that mediates between art and the world—between his internal aesthetic and external reality. In or around 1889 Seurat began painting abstract borders on the outside edges of the surface of the canvas that depict, as W. I. Homer and Niels Luning Prak have noted, Seurat's theory of color.[9] Dorra and Rewald claim that Seurat was so taken with the possibilities of these borders that he restretched most of the paintings in his studio and painted abstract borders around them.[10] Indeed, on some canvases that could not be restretched, Seurat painted borders over the perimeters of the picture itself, implying that his nonrepresentational frames were essential to his new conception of compositional space. Seurat was concerned with the polarity of artistic

8. Celant, "Framed: Innocence or Gilt?" 49.

9. W. I. Homer, "Seurat's Formative Period, 1880–1884," *Connoisseur* 162 (1958): 60; Niels Luning Prak, "Seurat's Surface Pattern and Subject Matter," *Art Bulletin* 53 (1971): 367–78.

10. Henri Dorra and John Rewald, *Seurat* (Paris: Les Beaux-Arts Editions, D'Etudes et de Documents, 1959), cii–ciii.

consciousness and the object of which it is conscious. The frame gave him a medium and a location for representation of perceiving consciousness, while the framed representational center included the objects perceived. The two modes of representation are distinct, thereby avoiding mutual penetration by (of) the pictorial and the abstract, which would at best synthesize the subjectivity-objectivity dialectic, and at worst compromise the aesthetic integrity of the artwork. The margins of the composition are expanded to acknowledge that both subjectivity and objectivity are intrinsic to the act of representation, but that they should exist as a duality, not an opposition or a synthesis. H. Peter Stowell, in *Literary Impressionism*, explains that objects represented in painting are functions of the consciousness viewing them; that consciousness, in turn, "acquires existence and meaning only in relation to the objects and events" perceived. Stowell calls the relationship a duality of "subjective-objectivity" (18). Seurat's use of the frame indicates an advance in the process begun by Degas: Seurat not only claimed the frame space, as Degas did; he used it to affirm the authority of his aesthetic vision and method.

Seurat's frames neither contain the semiotic field from outside nor simply demark it from within (as does, for instance, any composition that effectively ends before it reaches the borders of the canvas). Instead Seurat's frames represent the artistic consciousness that perceives and divides the endless aesthetic plane into compositional segments. Seurat and James have this in common: they believed that delineating a section of the aesthetic plane as a distinct semiotic field is an exercise of individual power. "The house of fiction," James says in the preface to *The Portrait of a Lady*, "has in short not one window, but a million—a number of possible windows not to be reckoned rather; every one of which has been pierced, or is still pierceable, in its vast front, by the need of the individual vision and by the pressure of the individual will" (3:x). Artistic vision is not only the plane's fabric, it is its design.

Seurat's abstract border frames integrated his theory and practice in a new way, calling into question the concept of a border between the artwork and the world. His borders, in effect, stretch the boundaries of the artwork to include the frame and to make the frame unique to, and constituent of, the composition; the method of composition is extended, for painting and frame share geometric design and color patterning. Yet the borders do not partake of the representational discourse associated with the pictorial. Although the painted borders are distinct, they are part of the aesthetic structure they demark. Furthermore, they suggest a continuing role for the artist in the completed work by constituting artistic consciousness, divested of the objects of sight, as it might exist when not in the act of perceiving.

In England, Dante Gabriel Rossetti, both poet and painter, sought in the frame a location for interartistic expression. Rossetti considered the frame as a discursive mediator between the world and the composition, and so used at least one of his frames to explicate the framed painting. As Alastair Grieve points out, on the frame originally designed by Rossetti for *The Girlhood of Mary Virgin* (1848), Rossetti inscribed two sonnets.[11] As W. M. Rossetti suggests, one sonnet explained the symbols of the artwork and the other related the artist's intentions.[12] Rossetti was concerned that his pictorial symbolism was too esoteric, and therefore would not be accessible to many viewers. Poetry, he must have reasoned, was more accessible or naturally more explicative than painting. The sonnets would educate the viewers to the syntax of the painting, and thereby inspire knowledgeable appreciation and greater value of the artwork.

Rossetti further adorned that frame with symbols identical to those on the canvas, thus extending the composition and explaining it in the same intermediary space. Rossetti was trying to establish a gradually less symbolic discourse that begins at the artwork's center and moves outward toward— perhaps including—the viewer. His frame does not represent abstract consciousness as Seurat's frames do; it rewrites the symbolized subject in another artistic language, and so the entire composition represents the artist as originator and interpreter, as creator and master of meaning. For Rossetti, "to emphasize the boundary means to point out art's specific concerns": he used the frame "to delineate a sacred enclosure,"[13] the value of which is not primarily economic or proprietary. Rossetti's use of the frame is insistently Romantic. He strongly suggests that his conception of the artist's relation to art, on the one hand, and to the spectator/reader, on the other, is spiritual in nature: like the priest or prophet, Rossetti mediates between meaning, which is metaphysical, and its relatively profane, physical representation in the world, attempting to create the ideal viewer by educating him or her to the aesthetics and iconography of his art. In his work, the chasm between art and the world, the inside and the outside of the frame, is bridged by performative

11. Alastair Grieve, "The Applied Art of Dante Gabriel Rossetti—I. His Picture-Frames," *Burlington Magazine* 115 (1978): 16–24.

12. W. M. Rossetti, *Dante Gabriel Rossetti, His Family Letters, with a Memoir* (London, 1915), 1:143, 2:45–46.

13. Celant, "Framed: Innocence or Gilt?" 31.

artistic consciousness, which claims unique powers of interpretation over the enclosed field. Moreover, the framing sonnet that expresses artistic intention implicitly attests that the origins of the artwork as they exist in the artist's memory are signified, though obliquely, in the work and, therefore, that total explication requires the agency of the consciousness that brought the work from origin to completion.

American artists of the late nineteenth century were influenced by circumstances similar to those influencing their contemporaries in Britain and France. American realism enjoyed great popularity, though the Realist writers and painters were frequently struggling to make ends meet. Imperialism, too, seemed integral to all three national characters. American territorial expansionism was driven by a lust for continental if not hemispheric control. Unlike those across the Atlantic, however, Americans were also struggling with the creation of a national identity and culture, to become empowered *within* national boundaries. Although Emerson's call in "Nature" to forget the past and seek national identity in the present went unheeded by those like Hawthorne, who found in the American past a rich source of literary material, others sought national identity in regional literatures, descriptions of local color, and monuments to American working heroes. The making of American art in the nineteenth century was redolent with the expansion of American culture. Similarly, the politics of framing in these movements were clearly dedicated to the expression and expansion of authority. In fact, the clearest relation of aesthetic form and political motive is the appropriation of the frame as a politicized border. Thomas Eakins, for example, adorned the frame of his portrait of Professor Henry A. Rowland with scientific formulas and the like in an effort to represent his subject in abstract discourse; one purpose of these framing adornments is to glorify Rowland's contributions to the sciences.[14] Eakins, like many of the Pre-Raphaelites, extended the semiotic discourse of the painting onto its border in an effort to control interpretation of the work and quite literally to extend his sphere of influence.

Like Eakins and these other nineteenth-century artists, James asserted his authority over the semiotic field by appropriating its border. For James, as we have seen, appropriation of the border ensured that the voice within that field would be utterly monologic: "there can be . . . only one truth and one direction—the quarter in which [the author's] subject most completely

---

14. On Eakins's portrait of Henry A. Rowland, see Henry Heydenryk, *The Art and History of Frames: An Inquiry into the Enhancement of Paintings* (New York: Heineman, 1963), 93.

expresses itself. The careful ascertainment of how it shall do so, and the art of guiding it with consequent authority—since this sense of 'authority' is for the master-builder the treasure of treasures, or at least the joy of joys— renews in the modern alchemist something like the old dream of the secret of life" (10:viii–ix). Clearly in this passage, and perhaps more baldly here than anywhere else in the prefaces, James reveals how the practice of art and the exercise of power are entwined. Aesthetic vision is totalitarian: it cannot tolerate competing versions of truth. The one truth and its expression are determined solely by "the master-builder" whose engineering transforms him into "the modern alchemist" with a primal desire to possess the ultimate power, eternal life. Yet the transformation from artisan to divinity requires the absolute authority that James must struggle to establish and maintain at the semiotic frontier.[15]

James's most elaborate defense of the semiotic border is his justification of the Edition's inclusion of A. L. Coburn's photographs as frontispieces. The photographs were to add appeal to the Edition, yet James thought that they, like all forms of illustration, would be perceived as supplementation, giving image to what, by definition, the text must be inadequate to present on its own. Illustration would "graft or 'grow' . . . a picture by another hand on my own picture," James says, and this would be nothing more than "a lawless incident" (23:ix). James would allow no competing voice to speak from the semiotic border about his text, for that voice would usurp his absolute authority.

James makes the issue a moral one: "Anything that relieves responsible prose of the duty of being, while placed before us, good enough, interesting enough, and, if the question be of picture, pictorial enough, above all *in itself,* does it the worst of services, and may well inspire in the lover of literature certain lively questions as to the future of that institution" (23:ix–x). Here again James asserts the impenetrability of an ideal text. Supplementation by another artist's aesthetic vision should not only be disallowed; it should not be possible. James admits that his concerns are derived from the growing picture-book industry in England and America, which he feared not only siphoned off potential readers, but created an entirely different sort of reader, one who would be little interested in James's work.[16] Yet his concern

15. Vivienne Rundle makes a similar argument in "Defining Frames: The Prefaces of Henry James and Joseph Conrad," *Henry James Review* 16 (Winter 1995): 66–92.

16. On the picture-book industry at the turn of the century, and on James's reactions to it, see Ralph F. Bogardus, *Pictures and Texts: Henry James, A. L. Coburn, and New Ways of Seeing in Literary Culture* (Ann Arbor: UMI Research Press, 1984).

derives from his fundamental notions of art, the duties of authorship, and the pleasures of reading:

> That one should, as an author, reduce one's reader, "artistically" inclined, to such a state of hallucination by the images one has evoked as does n't permit him to rest till he has noted or recorded them, set up some semblance of them in his own other medium, by his own other art—nothing could better consort than *that*, I naturally allow, with the desire or the pretention to cast a literary spell. (23:x)

The author should so captivate his reader that the reader cannot help trying to re-create the fictive world in drawing and other visual media. Yet James is anything but subtle as he reminds the reader that such re-creation is an *other* medium and an *other* art. It is related to, but absolutely distinct from the art to which it refers. They are, James says, nothing less than two distinct gardens tended and ruled over by two different gardeners.

Having established the rule that illustration can have no formal semiotic connection with his work, James becomes generous. "One welcomes illustration, in other words, with pride and joy." Yet he cannot bring himself to praise Coburn's work without once again defending his authority over the semiotic border: illustration is welcome,

> with the emphatic view that, might one's "literary jealousy" be deferred to, it would quite stand off and on its own feet and thus, as a separate and independent subject of publication, carrying its text in its spirit, just as that text correspondingly carries the plastic possibility, become a still more glorious tribute. (23:x)

In a brilliant move, James has transformed what he first considered a dangerous insult to his art into a "glorious tribute" to it. The trick of the illustrator seems to be deference to the author and to the integrity of his work. James must be allowed to maintain the perception that the photographs serving as frontispieces are absolutely "separate and independent" texts with no interpretive rights over James's text. They are not allowed to even "pretend to keep, anything like dramatic step with their suggestive matter," for to do so, to even pretend that they have any semiotic relation to James's novels and tales, "would quite have disqualified them" (23:x). Yet the photographs are inevitably read as part of the Edition and not some complementary text that accompanies it. Ralph Bogardus, whose *Pictures and Texts* is the most extensive consideration of the James-Coburn relation, claims that "the

Prefaces, the revised texts, and, finally, the beautiful frontispieces merge
to achieve a well conceived whole" (22). Bogardus concludes his study in
a way that would shock James: he reads the photographs and the novels
and tales as intertexts that not only refer to one another, but depend
upon one another for signification. His assumptions about the semiotic
integrity of the Edition, and of each volume in it, generally coincide with
those of the present study; however, Bogardus does not seem to recognize,
or he chooses to overlook, James's marked discomfort with the inclusion
of Coburn's photographs. That discomfort causes an abrupt discussion of
the photographs in the final preface, where one would expect James to
acknowledge implicitly or overtly the forthcoming extinction of the unique
voice of the prefaces with which he has been engaged for a few years.
James seeks to contain the photographs in language, to control Coburn's
referential vision by subjecting it to his proprietary discourse. Moreover,
as frontispieces (and not as intrusive illustrations), the photographs exist
outside the outermost frame of James's semiotic territory: they precede the
title and the announcement of authorship.

At the risk of sounding like a dilettante, James demands that his aesthetic
vision be sovereign; otherwise he risks losing his privilege and becoming
one of any number of readers trying to impose themselves on the text.
His sovereignty is derived from the idealization of his own reading, which
depends upon his unique position to the text. In his consciousness the
text was begun, and through his consciousness we will receive it. James
historicizes his relation to the artwork by embedding it in the history of
his consciousness in order to claim the authority of origins and, as has been
claimed recently by David McWhirter, to revivify the text, to make it a living,
organic reality rather than a sarcophagal entity that bespeaks completion
and authorial death.[17]

James's concern that the semiotic border be monologic clearly reiterates
the more problematized concerns of the preface to Hawthorne's *The Scarlet
Letter*, of which James was quite enamored.[18] Hawthorne seems ambivalent
about his authority, and so must create sources with which he can enter

17. McWhirter, "Introduction: 'The Whole Chain of Relation and Responsibility': Henry
James and the New York Edition," in *Henry James's New York Edition: The Construction of Authorship*,
ed. David McWhirter (Stanford: Stanford University Press, 1995), 1–19.

18. Recently, Hawthorne's readers have explored the framing relation of the preface and romance in *The Scarlet Letter*. See for example Nina Baym, "The Romantic Malgré Lui: Hawthorne
in 'The Custom-House,'" *ESQ: A Journal of the American Renaissance* 19 (1973): 14–25.

into dialogue before assuming authority over his text. In the "Custom-House" sketch, Hawthorne purports to trace the origin of his story to a found artifact, the scarlet A (that is ironically created in the narrative that it incites) and to the written history ascribed to it by Surveyor Pue, both of which are presumed to exist in the real (extraliterary) world before their textual representation in the fiction of the preface. The discovery of Surveyor Pue's history in the Custom-House attic and the subsequent examination of the red-cloth A that it encloses begins the transformation of the narration of history into a narration of romance; seeing it as "most worthy of interpretation," Hawthorne feels the "mystic symbol subtly communicating itself to [his] sensibilities, but evading the analysis of [his] mind."[19] Pue's history—albeit fictive—leads to the historicized sign of romance, the pulsating scarlet A. As McKeon points out in his general discussion of the discovered manuscript topos and its parodies, the commingling of history and fiction questions the veracity of the border that separates reality and romance; therefore, it implicates the instability of the semiotic border and the uncertainty of the power—the author—that rules there.[20] In fact, the history of Hawthorne's tenure at the Custom-House is made suspect when it becomes the background for the fantastic tale of the scarlet letter's discovery amidst Surveyor Pue's papers in the Custom-House attic.

Conversely, the "roll of dingy paper" that Hawthorne finds claims historicity for the romance that it spawns (28). Yet unlike James, who gives room for Coburn's photographs, Hawthorne never allows this second voice to intrude upon his text. Hawthorne doubly encloses Pue's history, first in the unexposed roll of paper, then in the Essex Historical Society archives, as if Pue's discourse were more threatening than fruitful to his romance. Nevertheless, Hawthorne cannot sever his work from its source—this alternate text—for in Hawthorne's mind Pue's document renders the story "authorized and authenticated" (29); it is a sign of truth.

Hawthorne uses the existence of Pue's version of Hester Prynne's story to empower himself as the author of fiction. The frame declares that the framed novel is Hawthorne's treatment of his impression: the result of much meditation, he says, of subjects that the frame either excludes (Pue's history) or invokes (the history of Hawthorne's ancestors, for example). The "Custom-House" preface eventually enables the author to claim unique

19. *The Scarlet Letter*, ed. Sculley Bradley et al. (New York: Norton, 1978), 28. All further references in this chapter will be cited in the text.
20. McKeon, *The Origin of the English Novel*, 56–57, 60, 182, 273–78.

authority over his text without saddling him with the responsibilities and implications of being the story's inventor.

As the reader is led closer to the fictional world, the author's identity gradually becomes more closely involved with his own fiction: he begins merely as an "editor, or very little more" and ends as the "Decapitated Surveyor" himself, author of these "posthumous papers" (7, 36). Hawthorne not only displaces history with romance; he ultimately displaces his invented source, Surveyor Pue. No longer paying tribute and deferring to an original delineator of Hester Prynne's history, Hawthorne assumes authority over the text by claiming ownership of it; as he does so, Hawthorne finds a more comfortable identity. No longer the Custom-House clerk, subordinate to immediate superiors and dependent on political patronage, and no longer the idler storyteller under the critical gaze of his colonizing ancestors, Hawthorne becomes "the scribbler of bygone days" (37), a phrase that might modestly describe either a historian or a romance novelist, both of whom authorize visions of the past. This process of empowerment inscribes the process begun by Degas and advanced by Seurat and Rossetti. Hawthorne gradually accepts responsibility for his aesthetic vision; as he does so, he demands the powers he associates with authorship. Yet as he acknowledges his identity as author, Hawthorne recognizes that as author he ceases to exist once the romance proper begins. In a sense, he is decapitated by the action of the frame, and the narrative, because it follows his semantic death, becomes posthumous.

James's reading and revising of Hawthorne, as Richard Brodhead has suggested, is central to his conception of the profession of authorship, for Hawthorne was James's foremost American literary precursor.[21] It is not surprising, then, that in his 1879 biography of Hawthorne for the English Men of Letters Series, James would crown the "Custom-House" preface as the best part of Hawthorne's best work.[22] The "Custom-House" preface deals poetically with many of the critical issues with which James himself would struggle in his writing of the New York Edition prefaces, issues endemic to the political nature of the semiotic border. Moreover,

---

21. On Hawthorne's influence on James, see Richard Brodhead, *The School of Hawthorne* (New York: Oxford University Press, 1986); and John Carlos Rowe, *The Theoretical Dimensions of Henry James* (Madison: University of Wisconsin Press, 1984).

22. Henry James, *Hawthorne* (London, Macmillan, 1879); repr. in *Henry James: Literary Criticism: Essays on Literature, American Writers, English Writers* (New York: Library of America, 1984).

in his reading of Hawthorne that the biography describes, James perceived that Hawthorne was a kindred spirit, not in his aesthetic of fiction or in his method of claiming authority over his text, but in his ambivalence toward the relationship between art and the world. In his preface to *The Scarlet Letter* Hawthorne squirms as he tries to avoid the label of either reader or writer by deconstructing the opposition, while James shifts uncomfortably as a writer of realist fiction who is indebted to his reading of Hawthorne's romances. And both are writing ostensibly about an Other (Hawthorne about his novel, James about Hawthorne) while both are consumed with representation(s) of the self.[23] Perhaps this is the most compelling evidence of their similar conflicts: both Hawthorne and James found it necessary and desirable to write self-empowering prefaces during the writing (Hawthorne) or the rewriting (James) of their greatest work.

23. Cornelia Pulsifer Kelly argues that the *Life of Hawthorne* marks a crucial change in James's career. "From now on the path of criticism and the path of fictional endeavor were to be widely separated. . . . Critic and novelist were now to be two persons. For some time they had been drifting apart. James the Critic emerged with the *Life of Hawthorne* in 1879. Meanwhile James the Novelist was slowly but surely coming into his own." *The Early Development of Henry James* (Urbana: University of Illinois Press, 1965), 256. Kelley's distinction between James the Critic and James the Novelist is overstated; nevertheless, it contributes to the argument that James viewed reading and writing as distinct but inseparable activities. In *The Theoretical Dimensions of Henry James* (Madison: University of Wisconsin Press, 1984), John Carlos Rowe expresses the sentiment most boldly by saying, "In many ways, *Hawthorne* might be considered a critical preface to the realization in *Portrait* of James's early aim to transume his predecessor, Hawthorne" (32). Although Rowe is establishing the field on which he will present a Bloomian reading of Hawthorne's influence on James, his carefully wrought argument clearly relates James's *reading* to his *writing*, and it relates his criticism to his fiction. Moreover, Rowe figuratively places the criticism-as-prewriting on the semiotic border—the preface.

3

TALES OF ORIGIN AND
JAMES'S AESTHETIC MEMORY

In his introduction to *The Art of the Novel*, R. P. Blackmur contends that each
of James's prefaces to the New York Edition of his novels and tales is "the
story of a story."[1] His simple description suggests an important strategy of
the prefaces: they create a history of James's fiction that begins and ends with
the author's reading of his own works. Of *The Turn of the Screw*, for example,
James says, "To have handled again this so full-blown flower of high fancy is
to be led back by it to easy and happy recognitions. Let the first of these be
that of the starting-point itself—the sense, all charming again, of the circle,
one winter afternoon, round the hall-fire of a grave old country house" where
someone told James the story of a haunting (12:xiv). James's rereading leads
him back to the scene of creation, where his imagination "winces as at the
prick" made by "the stray suggestion, the wandering word, the vague echo"
that becomes the "single small seed" of suggestion that eventually matures
into the New York Edition text (10:v). Nearly every preface begins with—one
might even say, is founded upon—this circular history: first, James engages
in a revisionary reading of the novel or tale as he considers it for inclusion
in the Edition; his reading uncovers the origin and his authorship of the
original text, which is then revised and reread by the author, who in response

---

1. *The Art of the Novel: Critical Prefaces by Henry James*, with an Introduction by Richard P.
Blackmur (New York: Charles Scribner's Sons, 1934).

writes the history that becomes the preface with which our reading begins. The goal of this strategy is to establish James's credentials as both creator and ideal consumer of his work. These histories repeatedly empower James as the only reader with sufficient historical knowledge and critical acumen to effect such a thorough reading of the novels and tales that they yield up not only their stories, but their very origins—the stories of their stories. Unlike the "Custom-House" preface to *The Scarlet Letter*, for example, in which Hawthorne uses the found-manuscript topos to claim historicity (and thereby value) for his romance by providing the illusion of extraliterary, tangible sources (the parchments of Surveyor Pue tucked away in the Essex County archives and the throbbing letter A in the Custom-House attic), James's prefaces claim the power of historical knowledge, to borrow Susan Mizruchi's phrase,[2] for their author, and confirm James's privileged relation to his work. And once James's privilege and authority are established, he can speak ex cathedra of his work, teaching the modern reader how to appreciate his art.

Yet in the decade before writing the prefaces James was engaged in a profound epistemological shift concerning the relation of history and fiction. As Roslyn Jolly explains, no longer convinced of his Victorian belief that the historiographical model for the novel is the best defense against charges first made in the eighteenth century that novels are fraudulent histories and that the novelist is nothing other than an artful liar, James at the turn of the century began to espouse the modernist view that prose fiction has essential value and must be judged by standards specific to the novel.[3] That is, the novel needs no defense except perhaps against the untutored reader, and that the art of the novel requires an art of literary criticism that is independent of standards applied to other forms of prose, most notably history. In "The Art of Fiction" (1884) James as Victorian allies the novelist and the historian, charging both "to represent and illustrate the past, the actions of men," and he asserts that the novel "must speak with assurance, with the tone of the historian." Jolly contends that "James's effort in delineating the task of the novelist as historian (and indeed, the effort of realism in general) is to make the relation between story and narrative appear to follow the same order in fiction as it does in history—

2. Susan Mizruchi, *The Power of Historical Knowledge: Narrating the Past in Hawthorne, James, and Dreiser* (Princeton: Princeton University Press, 1988).

3. Roslyn Jolly, *Henry James: History, Narrative, Fiction* (Oxford: Clarendon Press, 1993), esp. chaps. 1 and 6.

to reverse it, making the fictional narrative appear to be reporting events that have already taken place" (24–25), and so lending the credence of history to the art of the novel. By the end of the century, however, James was willing "to abandon the attempt to mount a philosophical defence of fiction against traditional charges of false epistemology" (195). "The Future of the Novel" (1899), in fact, prepares the way for the New York Edition by claiming no other or better justification for the novel than "some purely practical masterpiece." With this, according to Vivien Jones, "the conservative idealist and the modernist merge";[4] James steps into the twentieth century. James no longer required historiography to support his cause nor its standards to evaluate his work; in fact, in the prefaces he uses its method to liberate his work from the clutches of those readers still laboring under purely nineteenth-century Realist assumptions of literary critical practice, assumptions that James himself once endorsed and about which he was still very actively engaged in debate.

I do not mean to overstate the case. In the prefaces James does not empower his authorial voice by divesting his fiction of all connections with the extraliterary world.[5] Nor does he seek to remove the artwork from its social, historical, and cultural contexts. His prefatory reliance upon historical narrative suggests James's own belief in the power of historical knowledge. Mizruchi maintains that for James, "manipulations of temporal perceptions and historical narratives serve as means of empowering the self and dominating others. Shaping and reshaping" historical narratives, as James does in the prefaces, privileges the author and by extension, the in-doctrinated reader. Mizruchi explains, "James's works contain ruthless caste systems of historical consciousness, privileging those who consult memory in awareness of history's effects over those who inhabit an ahistorical void."[6] As James appropriates historical discourse to his own aesthetic ends, he enacts the continuous influx of the extraliterary into the literary world that

4. Vivien Jones, *James the Critic* (New York: St. Martin's, 1985), 6.
5. This claim counters most phenomenological readings of James. James's theory of the novel, particularly as it is expressed in the eighteen prefaces, is frequently read as soundly phenomenological, defining the novel as an expression of an "individual subject's total consciousness—especially in his relation to the world of objects. . . . Put between brackets and thus supposedly neutralized are all preexisting and thus 'metaphysical' significations, whether they be psychological, historical, social, or political." Carroll, *The Subject in Question: The Language of Theory and the Strategies of Fiction* (London: University of London Press, 1982), 10–11. See also Paul Armstrong, *The Phenomenology of Henry James* (Chapel Hill: University of North Carolina Press, 1983).
6. Mizruchi, *Power of Historical Knowledge*, 67.

accompanies reading. In the prefaces, historical discourse is not neutralized; all that constitutes the extraliterary is not stripped of significance. Instead, the aesthetic appropriation of the historical act of tracing origins signifies James's appreciation of the power of history and is his attempt to harness that power to his singular authorial presence. James evades neither history nor other extraliterary discourses; instead he uses them, transforms them to his own aesthetic ends, and naturalizes them in his fiction.

Yet the tales of origin cannot help calling James's role as creator into question; as historical narratives they locate the origin of his fiction in the extraliterary realm, where it is recovered through the author's personal, historical memory. Recalling the germ of an idea in a witnessed scene or actual situation, he appears to claim a prior real existence for each novel and tale and to portray the fiction as the aesthetic representation of that original state. The story in *The Turn of the Screw*, for instance, is presented in the preface as preexistent to *The Turn of the Screw* itself, which is then made to appear derivative. According to this logic, James is not the creator, but only the storyteller. Moreover, as the discourse of historical inquiry, by which I mean the attempted nonfictive recollection and interpretation of the past, the tales of origin not only seem to deny the originality of the text; they threaten to subvert James's formalist aesthetic of fiction by transforming the work into a signifying artifact of the historical discourses of James's autobiography and of the literary history that the prefaces relate. Once autobiography and literary history are written, the artifacts can be stored away; such is the fate of Hawthorne's imagined sources. In this sense, the discourse of historical inquiry that James employs conflicts with the ultimate goal of the prefaces: to create a formalist, aesthetic world that is hermetic, sovereign, and possessed by its creator as an object of his consciousness. Historical discourse claims authority for the extraliterary world in which it views literary discourse as an artifactual trace of that which it valorizes: the extraliterary origin that, as David Carroll argues, is "assumed to exist before its representation" in and as fiction.[7]

I would argue, however, that James's strategy of framing his fiction in a history of authorial conciousness that stretches from creation to James's ultimate consumption of his work does not describe the fictive worlds as reinventions of the textually exterior, historically defined world, even when the tales of origin locate and identify the "wind-blown germs" of his fictions

7. Carroll, *Subject in Question*, 88.

(3:viii). James employs the methods of historical inquiry to an end other than the production of history. In fact, the rhetoric of historical inquiry in the prefaces frequently does not lead to recovery and simple disclosure of the narratives' historical origins at all, but to a loss or suppression of origins. Of *The Tragic Muse*, for example, James admits, "I fail to recover my precious first moment of consciousness of the idea to which it was to give form; to recognise in it—as I like to do in general—the effect of some particular sharp impression or concussion" (7:v). In *Theoretical Dimensions*, John Carlos Rowe claims that failure to fully recover the origin is inevitable: "both the 'germ' and the 'central consciousness' undergo destabilization, even deconstruction, in the course of James's revisionary tour. . . . The 'germ' is never recoverable in such an act of supplementary" reading.[8]

The historicizing tales of origin simultaneously transform and retain the integrity of James's fiction by describing the work of fiction as exterior and antecedent to its tale of origin (as the source of its history) and as interior (as the object of discourse about and around which the tale of origin speaks).[9] The tale of origin, that is, comes into being through James's privileged reading of his work and does not rely on some artifact from the extraliterary world. Memory operating in the prefaces suppresses or devalues any extraliterary origin or state of the fiction that preexists the author's transformation of the real world into the world created in his art, and therefore it seems antihistorical. In the prefaces, James describes origin as the conception of fiction—of the world created—whereas that which precedes origin is merely an "alert recognition," an echo of the extraliterary world (12:v). The recognition that led to many of James's fictions of the international life, he says in the preface to "Lady Barbarina," is the oft-repeated tale of the young American woman who marries a European of position. Yet this is not the *origin* of the tale. As James says in the preface to *The Portrait of a Lady*, the origin of "the fictive picture" begins with "the vision of some person," with "my grasp of a single character" (3:vii, xi). In short, what is suggested in the outside world must be created by the author as an aesthetic object, and this creation is the origin of the artwork. In other words, James never takes us outside of Plato's cave. The flickering images

---

8. John Carlos Rowe, *Theoretical Dimensions of Henry James* (Madison: University of Wisconsin Press, 1984), 236.

9. Barbara Johnson calls this process *sublation,* "the traditional English translation of the German *Aufhebung,* which is Hegel's term for the simultaneous negation and retention of what is being surpassed by the process of dialectical thought." Barbara Johnson, ed. and trans., *Dissemination,* by Jacques Derrida (Chicago: University of Chicago Press, 1981), 4 n.

on the wall exist and are of value in their own right, apart from any relation to the objects passing by the cave entrance. "The fatal futility of Fact," James says, can be avoided, "once the seed [is] transplanted" from the extraliterary world. Yet in the process of transplantation, the seed, and consequently that which it produces, are utterly transformed. Historical reality must be reduced "almost to nought"; the remnant must be "washed free of awkward accretions and hammered into a sacred hardness," before the author can open his window on the aesthetic world (10:vii, v). James contends that the literary text does not speak directly of the extraliterary world, nor does it signify the history of that world: in Fredric Jameson's words, the text "speaks only of its own coming into being, of its own construction."[10] The memory that traces origin, then, is itself the *aesthetic memory* of what James calls the "seeking fabulist," the author engaged in literary creation. The moment that the suggestion of the extraliterary world sparks creation of the literary world, James as observer of the real life becomes James, the author of the fictive world and of aesthetic experience. The tales of origin, therefore, actually trace the origins of authorial consciousness as they locate the origins of fiction. They are tales of authorial origin and of the beginning of James's performance as an author.

This is why the tales of origin inevitably include James's memories of selecting the proper material for his fiction, transforming that material into the fabric of art, and carefully finishing the product: the history of the text and the history of the author are co-extensive. As Leo Bersani claims, "by moving from causes to composition . . . James insists on the fact that fictional invention is neither evasive nor tautological; instead, it constitutes the self": the world received and remembered is transformed into the world created, and this transformation both produces and requires authorial consciousness.[11] In truth, then, the tales of origin are not historical, antihistorical, or ahistorical; they are historicizing. James subverts the methods of historical inquiry by subordinating them to the creation and empowerment of authorial consciousness, which, as David Carroll claims, is in James's work both "the definitive origin" and the very "center of the novel" itself.[12] The prefaces provide that consciousness with its own narrative existence as it perceives itself in the act of creating the text and, ultimately, of

10. Fredric Jameson, *The Prison-House of Language: A Critical Account of Structuralism and Russian Formalism* (Princeton: Princeton University Press, 1972), 89.

11. Leo Bersani, *A Future for Astyanax: Character and Desire in Literature* (New York: Little, Brown, 1969), 132.

12. Carroll, *Subject in Question*, 56.

reading it. They are the record of James's aesthetic memory as it is signified in the prefaced novels and tales. To examine the implications of James's delineation of the conflict between the logic of history and the logic of fiction, we need look closely at two novels and their prefaces, *The Aspern Papers* and *The Awkward Age*. The preface to *The Aspern Papers* discloses the historical correlative of James's plot; whereas in the preface to *The Awkward Age*, no such disclosure is forthcoming. Each preface prepares the reader for the conflict as it is dramatized in the prefaced novel. In all the prefaces, however, James relies on historical knowledge and narrative strategies as sources of power while claiming that truth and accuracy to historical facts are burdens under which no novelist can labor successfully. The synthesis between these two ostensibly conflicting positions is the aesthetic memory that informs the prefaces. A brief look at the preface to *The Portrait of a Lady* will illustrate my point.

It is often said that history does not tell us who we are, but who we would like to be. Aesthetic memory allows James to craft historical narrative— one might even say to create history—that best helps satisfy his desire for authorial power and that best complements the fiction that it describes: aesthetic memory speaks the truth of beauty rather than the beauty of truth. From the first sentence of the preface to *The Portrait of a Lady*, James begins creating an identity for the text by constructing a contextualizing history that, though not historically accurate, is conceptually appropriate. " 'The Portrait of a Lady' was, like 'Roderick Hudson,' begun in Florence, during three months spent there in the spring of 1879" (3:v). After a brief account of the novel's simultaneous, trans-Atlantic serialization in the *Atlantic Monthly* and *Macmillan's Magazine*, James continues: "It is a long novel, and I was long in writing it; I remember being again much occupied with it, the following year, during a stay of several weeks made in Venice" (3:v). These first few facts attending the tale of origin are misleading. James says in his notebooks, which he consulted while writing the prefaces, that *Portrait* was indeed begun in Florence, but then he corrects himself: "that is, I took up, and worked over, an old beginning, made long before."[13] The old beginning is suppressed in the preface because James prefers to provide the novel with an origin more closely associated with Italy, the landscape of Isabel Archer's destiny.[14] This

13. *The Notebooks of Henry James*, ed. F. O. Matthiessen and K. B. Murdock (Oxford: Oxford University Press, 1947), 29.

14. Charles Feidelson notes this omission from the preface, but makes no comment on it. Instead, Feidelson discusses James's ascription of "the long gestation of the book" to "the

careful manipulation of historical narrative results in the implication that *Portrait* is a representation of that of which the author was aware at the time of conception and writing, and this context, lodged in the frame, becomes a determining factor in the semiotics of the novel (a proposition I return to in Chapter 6).

James does not imply in the preface that the ability to suppress an old and "true" beginning suggests the possibility of ultimate self-creation. In fact, he suggests the reverse. In the "fruitless fidget of composition," unable to continue without the help of some external catalyst, he continually went to the window of his Venetian study for inspiration. He relied on the world outside himself, outside his study, to correct and contribute to his inner vision: "the wondrous lagoon spread before me, and the ceaseless human chatter of Venice came in at my windows, to which I seem to myself to have been constantly driven, in the fruitless fidget of composition, as if to see whether, out in the blue channel, the ship of some right suggestion, of some better phrase of the next happy twist of my subject, the next true touch for my canvas, might n't come into sight" (3:v). Altering the history of *Portrait*'s origin, James implies that history is a contextualizing agent that, like all contextualizing agents, provides identity: the history of *The Portrait of a Lady* that he chooses to relate (whether historically accurate or not) helps provide an identity for that novel that he elects for it after, and as a result of, his reading of it.

As his reliance on, and manipulation of, historical narrative suggests, James's ambivalent use of historicizing tales of origin is informed by an understanding of preface and prefaced text as a complex semiotic field, the internal logic of which depends primarily upon the aesthetic concerns of the fiction to which James as idolized author and idealized reader would have his readers attend. Tracing origins is essential to James, not only because it empowers him as the privileged reader who uncovers the process of composition, but also, he contends, because without "such remembered glimmers . . . comes no clear vision of what one may have intended, and without that vision no straight measure of what one may have succeeded in doing" (7:v). Without framing his text with a recovery of its origin, James believes, he cannot be assured that the reader can evaluate the text

---

slightness of the single character that gave him his start"—Isabel Archer (742). Feidelson follows the pattern James establishes in the preface of deferment of the novel's origin to other satellite topics. See "The Moment of *The Portrait of a Lady*" *Ventures* 8, no. 2 (1968): 47–55.

accurately for the reader will have no literary critical tools appropriate to the text at hand. Implicitly, it is James himself who will be the subject of the evaluation. Whether the artist has achieved his goal or not is significant only if the text is to be considered the ground of artistic endeavor. The prefatory tale of origin, therefore, begins the transformation of the prefaced text into the self-conscious art object that will signify the powers of its author and exemplify the standards by which the novel should be judged.

In James's oeuvre, *The Aspern Papers* is the work most concerned with the methods and ethics of literary historiography; not surprisingly, therefore, both preface and prefaced text consider and distinguish the logic employed by the historian and the logic of the seeking fabulist. Although James claims that he fears his apparent ingenuity of invention will be unmasked as happy circumstance and merely the change of names, he begins this preface with a bold recovery of narrative origins. He recalls in some detail the history of Jane Clairmont, Lord Byron, Percy Shelley, and an American scholar— the historical correlative of his tale of the Aspern scholar. Describing these events, James seemingly invites comparison between the real and the fictive narratives. Recovering the historic narrative in the preface and recovering it in the fiction establishes by implication the contrast between historic and aesthetic structures of reality. The preface, in fact, extensively examines the difference between history and art, particularly how each uses the past. Historical consciousness depends upon verifiable factual knowledge as its source of authority. Facts and artifacts are crucial to the promulgation of historical narrative: they are its palpable origins and signs of its authenticity and value. The fabulist, on the other hand, eschews factual knowledge and creates his or her own fount of truth: aesthetic vision. "The minimum of valid suggestion serve[s] the man of imagination better than the maximum. The historian, essentially, wants more documents than he can really use; the dramatist only wants more liberties than he can really take" (12:vii); this is for James the crucial difference between aesthetic and historic logics.

James, unlike the antiquarian who "wakes up in time" to become Miss Clairmont's pensionnaire and object of her yearning in hopes of a bequest of rare Shelley documents, had no desire to visit the woman who overlapped literary epochs. The literary historian lusted after the documents, the germs of potential historical discourse, for they would establish his authority: she or he who possesses the documents possesses the origin of historic narrative. Without control of them, the literary historian risks encountering rival dis- courses, rival narratives that may overpower and supplant his own. Adhering to the logic and value system of history, Hawthorne initially attributes his romance to Surveyor Pue's script and to the artifactual A, over which he has control. But the fabulist, James says, desires only an impression, the possibility of narrative and not the verifiable, artifactual origin. "Nine tenths of the artist's interest in [facts] is that of what he shall add to them and how he shall turn them" (12:ix). Neither Miss Clairmont, who lived in Florence when James visited there, nor the Shelley papers she may have possessed, were of interest as artifacts to James's impressionable, authorial consciousness. On the contrary, it was "the thrill of learning that she 'overlapped' [the previous epoch and his own], . . . and the wonder of my having doubtless at several earlier seasons passed again and again, all unknowing, the door of her house," James says, that gave him all he desired (12:viii). In his or her dealings with the world, the fabulist seeks active states of consciousness, not possession of historical objects as such.

Presentation of the history of Jane Clairmont and the deceiving yet desired scholar might threaten James's authority. The historically informed reader might read *The Aspern Papers* in the light of his own knowledge of the past, interpret the text according to what he knows has been suppressed by the author, and so gain power over the author by translating *The Aspern Papers* into his own duplicitous narrative of historical suppression. Recognizing the threat that such a co-optive reading presents to his authority, James makes a preemptive strike, preventing the subsumption of his work into historical narrative by subsuming the history into his own frame of aesthetic reference. James profits by the revelation, in fact, because he establishes a contrast between the historical narrative, which was "rich" but "dim," and *The Aspern Papers*, which casts the transforming aesthetic light upon "things absolutely sealed and beyond test or proof" (12:viii). James demonstrates, in other words, that he can make an elaborate narrative world with semiotic integrity in the realm of the sacred out of the meager offerings of largely unrealized historical narrative of the profane world.

The preface to *The Aspern Papers* is a meditation on the desire for authority gained by knowledge of the past. And the past fascinates James, the "palpable imaginable visitable past" (12:vii). Here too the fabulist's fascination is distinguished from the historian's unreserved yearning for artifactual, verifiable, resuscitation of the past. Both the historian's and the fabulist's desires for historical knowledge are desires for the essence of narrative, that which can appropriate, control, and nurture the past within its well-crafted structure. James desires the past to be palpable so that he may take hold of it, bring it "almost to nought" and then hammer it into the sacred hardness that is the origin of art. Unlike the antiquarian who objectifies texts (documents) into historical artifacts, James seeks to make real—to make tangible—ideas of the past. By shaping what has been, James gains considerable control over the present.

The analogy James chooses to express this conception of the past is significant to his discussion in the preface and the prefaced narrative's enactment of his concepts. James portrays history as a series of framed structures, the contents of which are partially assumed (based on the historian's temporal environs), partially seen, and partially invented. Historical knowledge is described as subjective, relative to the historian's relation to the past.

> With more moves back [in historical time] the element of the appreciable shrinks—just as the charm of looking over a garden-wall into another garden breaks down when successions of walls appear. The other gardens, those still beyond, may be there, but even by use of our longest ladder we are baffled and bewildered—the view is mainly a view of barriers. The one partition makes the place we have wondered about other, both richly and recogniseably so, but who shall pretend to impute an effect of composition to the twenty? (12:x)

Looking backward in time ultimately is futile because only the outlines of epochs are discernible. The past can be known only in reference to the present, which is itself another walled enclosure. So for James, the desire for historical truth is fated to burn without fulfillment. Even the perceived structures of history, the succession of garden walls, are too vast to be understood from any human perspective. Therefore, what can be known is only what can be imagined; and this holds true, James suggests, for both the seeking fabulist and the historian. For James the implications are clear. Whereas the nineteenth-century novelist was judged by standards derived from tools meant to evaluate the accuracy and strength of historical narrative, the twentieth-century historian might well find himself judged on his ability to imagine, that is, by standards and evaluative tools designed for the novelist. Moreover, while the analogy of the succession of garden walls establishes the garden as a physical manifestation of this desire for control of history, it also implies the need to remain enclosed and safe from intrusions by both the past and the future. A wall, like a frame, is both inside and out. The metaphor also implicates James's presentation of origin of the fictive picture as a seed. The enclosed garden, it seems, is the turf of the fabulist.

The desire for knowledge of the past is pervasive in the preface and in the prefaced narrative. James grasps his historical objects and climbs his

longest ladder because he senses a power that is inherent in knowledge of
the other (be it the past, or indeed another individual). He will not inhabit
an ahistorical void, in other words; he will reach beyond his temporal frame
and he will admit the other into his frame only through his consciousness
of it. "We are divided of course between liking to feel the past strange and
liking to feel it familiar," James says; "the difficulty is, for intensity, to catch it
at the moment when the scales of the balance hang with the right evenness"
(12:x). History to be appropriated is history that is neither too pungently
immediate nor too diffused and distant. Aesthetic memory creates a sense
of the past; it does not seek to re-create the past as historic memory would.
James passes over the temporal frames imaginatively, not physically, and so
the palpable past is in fact his own creation, his own consciousness of the
past manifested in narrative.

According to James, the historian seeks full control over the veritable
past by re-presenting it in the present. Therefore, when a person or object
survives the closing of one epoch and the opening of the next—as James
did—that survivor is of particular antiquarian interest. Miss Clairmont, for
example, was herself a relic from a previous era. Her memories were precious
but, more importantly to the Shelley scholar, her very existence promised
the existence of documents and artifacts that would originate and authenti-
cate historical narrative. They would allow the scholar to reshape the present
conception of that past, and with control over those singular objects, he
alone would have the authority to reshape it.

More interesting to James, however, is consideration of what the present
thinks of the past, not an attempt to reproduce the past empirically. Aesthetic recovery is offered by the preface to *The Aspern Papers* as the moral
and successful alternative to appropriation of the other (and the other's
possessions) and the consequent dependence on those relics for narrative
authority. James took possession of the "dim Shelley drama" from history by
transforming his impression of it into his own aesthetic structure: "I 'took
over,' as I say, everything that was of the essence, I stayed my hand for
the rest" (12:ix). James did not appropriate the tangible evidences of the
history, not even the sight of Miss Clairmont, whom he carefully avoided.
He divested the history of its annoying factual attributes, forged it into
the sacred hardness at the origin of art, and composed a text of his own
aesthetic vision.

In this prefacing adventure of aesthetic appropriation of history, James
is the protagonist, expressing a fierce desire for a historical consciousness.
He sets the example that is always lurking behind the antiquarian's story of

his own Italian journey, providing both the moral and the interpretive keys to the succeeding text. Origin, James implies, is necessary to authority. But the origin of narrative fiction, unlike the origin of narrative history, need not depend upon the author's possession of relics that signify its historic correlative. Again, the metaphoric language of the tales of origin enforces this distinction: the writer of fiction begins with a seed, which bespeaks conception, while the writer of history begins with the relic, which suggests mortification. The furtive desire to create—to imagine a past, in this case, and not to consume it—is the power that ignites the origin of fiction. However, like Hawthorne in the "Custom-House" preface, the antiquarian in *The Aspern Papers* is neither completely a historian nor completely a seeking fabulist. He commingles (sometimes badly and sometimes effectively) the logics of both methods of shaping the past.

As the narrator of his own history, the Aspern scholar functions as an author who represents his subject (himself) as a historian. The consciousness of the subject filters the world inhabited by the Bordereaus; the consciousness presented in the narrative filters the memory of that world and, we discover at the end, that recovery of its own past is influenced by objects in the world in which he writes. He is a Jamesian character through and through, a sensitive register of every vibration made in his strangely anachronistic world. Yet he is also a historian, and as such he distrusts subjectivity and seeks objectification of the past through possession of relics from a previous era. As a historian, the narrator depends upon the portrait of Jeffrey Aspern that hangs above his writing table. This portrait, however, like all historical relics once the logic of historical inquiry has been abandoned for the logic of aesthetic re-covery, signifies loss of authority to the narrator: "When I look at it I can scarcely bear my loss—I mean of the precious papers" (12:143). The narrator, acting like a fabulist but thinking like a historian, is conveying his sense of a past in which he lost the opportunity to control the shaping of historical knowledge. His entire narrative records the loss of the objectifiable past and its inevitable replacement by relativist, subjective "Jamesian history"—the actual is replaced by subjective consciousness of it.

As a historian, the Aspern scholar cannot, like James, be content with either the knowledge that the letters existed or the impression made by the knowledge that Aspern's Juliana lived into his own era. He must surround himself with artifacts in order to authorize his knowledge of the past. Yet he is historicizing falsely. The narrator projects himself into the past without the interpretive tools of either the formal historian or the autobiographer.

The narrator and his subject are too frequently inseparable for any pretence of objectivity.[15]

The doubled consciousness of the Aspern scholar, as retrospective narrator and as engaged subject, sometimes confuses rather than clarifies the past. For example, when commerce between himself and the two Miss Bordereaus is suspended shortly after his admission into their house, the antiquarian stops sending flowers to their rooms, which instantly provokes Miss Juliana to call for a meeting. He imagines she is either reacting to information passed on by her niece, Miss Tina, that he is an Aspern scholar, or to the absence of his bouquets. The subject that is broached first by Miss Bordereau is the garden. The subject consciousness reads this as a reaction to the flowers (or lack thereof); the retrospective narrator sees this as one gesture of a more complex move on Juliana's part to control her tenant and get the most out of him. The reader doesn't know which version of the past, if either, to believe.

Fortunately, the preface provides another frame of reference that places the scene in the context of the conflict between historical and aesthetic logics. The scholar entreats the elder Miss Bordereau to "'Come into the garden yourself and pick [the flowers]; come as often as you like; come every day. The flowers are all for you'" (12:71). As the preface has established it, the garden signifies engagement with historical knowledge. To invite Miss Bordereau into the garden of his design—the garden she ironically (and suggestively) let go to seed—is to coax her into his historical structure, to secure her within the frame of his own epoch, over which he seeks control. The flowers are signs of his will-to-historical-power over the potential historical narrative. Moreover, they are, paradoxically, signs of his desire to author fiction. The garden was rejuvenated by the scholar's imaginative sense of the past. He imagined what sort of garden would attract the lover of Jeffrey Aspern and what seductive messages would be read into his horticultural devotion, and then he proceeded to create in the present an imagined garden from the past based on his imagination and not on any specific factual knowledge.

15. Susanne Kappeler notes this ellision of narrator and subject in her discussion of *The Aspern Papers*. The critical reader of the Aspern scholar's tale, she claims, will begin to distance him- or herself from the "readymade values that were slipped in [by the narrator] from the beginning," and to wonder if the Aspern scholar's enterprise is indeed noble. Ultimately the reader must look for surer ground on which to stand, and the reader finds that ground not in the narrative provided by the Aspern scholar but in the signs of James's authorship—the title and preface. *Writing & Reading in Henry James* (New York: Columbia University Press, 1980), 24.

From the beginning, the garden is the locus of the Aspern scholar's aspirations to author fiction. He transforms the garden, the imaginative re-creation of the past that he claims to seek objectively, into a very immediate, experiential vehicle for his present authorial desires. While his first plan of initial approach was to offer the Bordereaus money for lodging, he admits that "the other idea that had come into my head was connected with a high blank wall which appeared to confine an expanse of ground on one side of the house. Blank I call it, but it was figured over with patches that please a painter, repaired breaches, crumblings of plaster, extrusions of brick that had turned pink with time; while a few thin trees, with poles of certain rickety trellises, were visible over the top. The place was a garden and apparently attached to the house. I suddenly felt that so attached it gave me my pretext" (12:10–11). Scaling the wall into the epoch that Miss Juliana and, by implication, Jeffrey Aspern, inhabit is the scholar's initial goal. The wall is an attractive artistic property; furthermore, it would "please a painter" and therefore seems to cry out for a seeking fabulist, not a historian. This fabulist the scholar becomes and, through the process of his various fictions, the objects for which he so yearns are lost to the unreachable past.

The garden that the scholar succeeds in creating is the scene of his seduction of Miss Tina—that for which he is morally culpable. It is also the source of his initial communications with the elder Miss Bordereau: the flowers that he produces in the garden are daily signifiers (to him, of his desire for the historical artifacts; to Miss Juliana Bordereau, that she has a source of desired income; to Miss Tina, that he might be a potential lover) that are both aesthetic and artifactual. He understands that such objects, created by the active imagination, give him great control over the present: not only can he control what they mean; he can leave their meaning indeterminate and therefore possibly multiple. He does not, however, appreciate the implications of the powers of the imagination. He continues to rely on objects for the meaning of his (historical) narrative rather than allow objects to rely on his narrative for meaning and existence. The scholar even builds an arbor in the garden that he hopes will attract Miss Bordereau, or perhaps her niece, who is a better intermediary, certainly, than the flowers. These objects are the origins and the media of the scholar's discourse.

Dependence on verifiable historical truth, objectified through artifacts, is the downfall of the scholar. Yet his authorial imagination, which seeks to divest itself of historical artifacts, has the power to survive the conflict and fully displace the historian's sensibility. The scholar repeatedly fends off the jarring dissimilarity between the Juliana he had imagined when reading Aspern's poetry and the Juliana Bordereau who appears so un-Romantic and relentlessly greedy. His imagination, in this instance, proves more potent than his historical sense; the scholar manages to disregard the disturbing discourse of reality and to transform present experience so that it conforms with his preferred sense of the past. But the narrator continually juxtaposes the empirical scholar's perceptions of Juliana Bordereau and his wildly divergent and persistent preconceptions of her. He seems to be suggesting that the present, like the past, is always a combination of individual, subjective experience of the world and of desires for the power that comes from shaping and reshaping those experiences. Even at the end, when the scholar returns to the palazzo to see Miss Tina one last time, his desire for the papers allows him to reinvent her, to believe that she has forgiven him and has subsequently been transformed: "She stood in the middle of the room with a face of mildness bent upon me, and her look of forgiveness, of absolution, made her angelic. It beautified her; she was younger; she was not a ridiculous old woman. This trick of her expression, this magic of her spirit, transfigured her" (12:141–42). As he was able to do with the aunt, so too with the niece. In fact, the scholar was less surprisingly able to maintain a conception of Aspern's valor and moral presence in the face of mounting evidence to the contrary. In every case his authorial desire at least temporarily overcomes his historical desire.

The tension between the Aspern scholar's desires for the powers afforded by the imagination and the powers of historical narrative is nowhere so clearly represented as his one dubious concession to what he himself singles out as "historical truth" (as if the surrounding narrative was truth of another sort): upon first seeing Miss Tina after her aunt's death, he claims, "But historic truth compels me to declare that his poor lady's dull face ceased to be dull, almost ceased to be plain, as she turned it gladly to her late aunt's lodger. That touched him extremely, and he thought it simplified his situation until he found it didn't. I was as kind to her that evening as I knew how to be, and I walked about the garden with her" (12:123). Historical discourse jars his authorial imagination so severely that the narrator slips into the third person, objectifying his subject (himself) as history demands. The representation of his emotions frightens him into the loss of subjective consciousness. When the threat recedes, history does as well, and the aesthetic imagination regains control. He recounts his attempt to gain control over Miss Tina by leading her from the house (the structure she controls) to the garden (his place of power).

Miss Juliana's relation to historical artifacts is not as different from the scholar's as one might at first assume. Like him, she wishes to control through possession of artifacts. And Miss Juliana's insistence on the sole possession of the papers, the artifacts that the scholar tells Miss Tina " 'would be of such immense interest to the public, such immeasurable importance as a contribution to Jeffrey Aspern's history,' " is her undoing (12:82). The elder Miss Bordereau seems at first to be an author figure. She has the desire to remain undisturbed just as James wanted to remain undisturbed by Miss Clairmont. She wants to control commerce between the world and her possessions just as James desires control over the relationship between his narrative and Miss Clairmont's history. Yet Miss Juliana has no desire to transform the objects she possesses by reducing them to some sacred hardness that will become narrative of her own vision. Her imagination is perhaps furtive, but completely infertile. Her weak attempts to lure the scholar into a marriage with her niece demonstrate her inability to control the narrative that exists within her own frame—her home.

In spite of her relatively weak powers to control, she fiercely resists becoming an authorial property. She shuns historical narratives of Aspern because she has no desire to become herself an artifact of historical discourse nor does she wish her own memories and the signs of her life (the papers) to be consumed by history. She no longer reads the papers as she used to, and therefore she is not dependent upon them to maintain a connection with her past (perhaps that connection is no longer important, or perhaps the blandness of her present has allowed the past to reassert itself without the assistance of the letters). Her desire for absolute and unique possession of the documents is her desire for power and, in a sense, for existence. Her personal relationship with Aspern that the papers reveal, if made public, would become itself a historical artifact and would be subsumed by a narrative controlled by the historian, not her. She had no desire to be displaced by her own history. Furthermore, by transferring the letters to the scholar, she would experience the death of the beloved poet once again: Aspern would be replaced by the published letters, which themselves would be subsumed in the critical history that they would incite. Perhaps this, too, explains why Miss Bordereau seemed to know little about critical histories of Jeffrey Aspern: they threatened to be the undoing of her relation to the past.

Like the scholar, Miss Juliana plays falsely. She risked the powers and responsibilities of authorship (historical and aesthetic) by using her own associations with the past to stockpile money. Her motives seem fair enough: she hoped to provide Miss Tina with a sizable legacy. However, she played as dishonestly as her adversary. She tried to convert the scholar's desire for her property into a future for her niece but never took into account his own authorial powers. She could not control him as thoroughly as she assumed. Her greed for control of the disposition of personal history disallowed her to settle any benefit it might bring on her niece. As a result, she did not produce any lasting narrative or legacy. Miss Bordereau's past might have provided a future for Miss Tina. It did not. It might have contributed a new narrative to the history of Jeffrey Aspern. It did not. Historical knowledge became for her a curse of self-consuming desire.

Miss Tina's relation to historical knowledge and her experience of the power of the imagination are nebulous at best. What she knows about her aunt's history is never fully ascertained by the scholar, and she has little desire either to purge or to develop whatever knowledge she does have. Miss Tina's meeting with the scholar in the garden signifies her entry into his frame of authority, but she incorrectly reads it as the frame of her own epoch, not of his imaginative combinations of past and present, of memory and desire. And while she seems to understand her aunt's authorial strategies, she does not fully comprehend her perceived paramour's manipulations until she herself attempts to initiate a narrative that would subsume him. She has no historical sense and therefore can be used both by her aunt, to help lure money from the scholar, and by the scholar, to help lure the papers from her aunt. Her authorial will is weak, asserting its desire only as a plea.

Only James speaks with the voice of reason, distinguishing the logics of history and fiction, and maintaining the marked distinction between what he has imagined of the past and what actually occurred in a previous era. The preface traces the origin of the narrative to a historical event, but then displaces that event by the process of its appropriation. The relation of history devolves into a discussion of the uses of historical knowledge, of what can be truly known about the past, and finally about how that knowledge can be appropriated successfully. James says that in the end, the question is not whether one has constructed narrative that is true to life. "One's warrant," James says, "hangs essentially on the question of whether or no the false element"—which is the element that is true within the fictive world but that does not have a direct, historical correlative in the extraliterary world—"imputed would have borne the test of further development which so exposes the wrong and so consecrates the right. My last word was, heaven forgive me, that, occasion favouring, I could have perfectly 'worked out' " that false element (which, in this case, is the creation of a distinguished early American literary presence). Truth to the fabulist is sometimes a falsehood to the historian. The standards may not differ, but the structures within which those standards apply most frequently do.

In the preface to *The Awkward Age,* James seems just as consumed with questions of history, but his approach to them is quite different: he represses and suppresses the essential elements of this tale of origin. James concedes that "this composition, as it stands, makes, to my vision . . . so considerable a mass beside the germ sunk in it and still possibly distinguishable, that I am half-moved to leave my small secret undivulged" (9:v). His admission that the seed and the already overgrown plant coexist throws the organic metaphor into question. Paradoxically, James says that the prefaced fiction has a "quantity of finish" in spite of the disturbing presence of the seed that he discovers in his revisionist reading (9:vi): it is both a fully finished work of art and the hammered, sacred hardness that is the origin of a work of art. James seems to fear the historical origin of the text, as if, like an instigating and suddenly recovered intention that little influences present actions, it would undermine the character and quality of those actions were it to come to light. The quantity and quality of "finish" James attributes to the prefaced text stave off threats of the intrusion of historical origin with evidences of aesthetic authority. Contrary to the expectations that the figure of the narrative as overgrown plant establishes, James does not focus on the unchecked, purportedly unseen development of plot from seed to maturation, even though emphasis of development might deflect attention from the all-too-present origin to authorial performance. In fact, James brings to the foreground a disjunction between origin and finished narrative that leaves development in the murky shadows of unrepresented authorial consciousness: James claims that *The Awkward Age* is monstrous, following "an unforeseen principle of growth" (9:v).

James neither produces nor ignores the origins that he claims to remember but refuses to disclose. Instead he introduces the threat of displacement of the present by residual signs of the past into the dynamic of reading. The threat becomes part of the fabric of the narrative and a frame of reference by which much of the narrative can be understood as a struggle for authority among the circle of those who seek control of the present—especially Mrs. Brookenham, her daughter Nanda, her sister the Duchess, and her mother's unsuccessful admirer Mr. Longdon. Each takes a narrative object, attempts to erase or suppress its historic reality or natural process of growth, and then aesthetically recover its "history" and present reality; in addition, each seeks a reader. The Duchess keeps her ward, Aggie, a blank of purity but constantly diverts attention to her own authorizing, not to her "text"; it is not Aggie's innocence, but the Duchess's skill at keeping her innocent that is remarked upon by those about her. Longdon tries to divest Nanda of what he perceives as the historical discontinuity created by the existence of her mother by bridging the generations, grandmother and granddaughter, that appear strikingly similar. Yet he is too clearheaded to truly blind himself to Nanda's forceful presence. Mrs. Brookenham authorizes in every direction (and frequently about Nanda) and so is ultimately ineffective. She never completely covers history with her aesthetic logic and never transplants the historic seed in the shallow soil of her imagination, and so she is constantly finding that the seeds of her would-be narratives are all too distinguishable and threaten to sprout simultaneous, independent narratives.

The story begins as the eldest of its characters, Mr. Longdon, like the author in the preface, bridges past and present by his singular awareness of its continuity. Spying a photograph of Nanda Brookenham, whom he has yet to meet because her mother, Mrs. Brookenham, meticulously keeps Nanda absent, Mr. Longdon immediately notices the resemblance between Nanda Brookenham and her late grandmother, Lady Julia; his consciousness constructs a temporal connection that can otherwise be effected only by comparing artifacts—pictures of the two women. The considerably younger Vanderbank, as reader of Longdon's encounters with the pictures, admits his lack of historical continuity but recognizes Longdon's knowledge as such:

> "I never saw Lady Julia, and you had in advance all the evidence I could have: the portrait . . . and the three or four photographs you must have noticed with it at Mrs. Brook's. These things must have compared themselves for you with my photograph in there of the granddaughter. The similarity of course we had all observed, but it has taken your wonderful memory and your happy vision to put into it all the detail." (9:145)

Like the author, Longdon has the privileged consciousness: he can discern in the pictures what others cannot; his memory can recover in full what others can scarcely imagine. Of course it is precisely this vision of the continuity of past and present that at first rejects similarity and elects displacement. At first Longdon spins alternate narratives based on the originating seed, Lady Julia (really, the impression she had made on him) rather than recalling the process of familial generation that resulted in Nanda—a process that would affirm Nanda's difference from (especially temporal), not her similarity to, her grandmother. Initially, Longdon is a historian like the Aspern scholar who observes past and present artifacts and seeks to control the present narrative, gaining authority over it by controlling knowledge of its origins. Longdon's mental possession of history incites him to feel empowered and entitled to control the present and hence to reshape and revise Nanda into a young revision of his unrequited love, Lady Julia. Fortunately, he learns to distinguish past and present as similar and contiguous but not identical. The origin and the originated only resemble one another; they are not duplicates.

Vanderbank, on the other hand, does not go beyond or behind the artifacts to author the present or to displace aesthetic with historic truth. Instead he focuses on the artifacts themselves and the impressions they make on others: of the cigarette case he shows to Nanda, Vanderbank says, " 'Its origin's lost in the night of time—it has no history except that I've used it' " (9:209). He is the phenomenological reader, who perceives only that which is presented to him and brackets everything else by defining objects according to use or impression rather than history or narrative potential. Impressions do not incite in him the authorial will-to-power. He submits willingly to the perceptions of those who demonstrate authorial power because he has no historical sense, nor aesthetic ability capable of appropriation if he had.

The threat of the historical past is translated in part in the narrative into the threat of previous generations to reappear and displace the present generation. Identity becomes contingent on one's place in an undisturbed succession; therefore, present relations are affected by uncertain, unimpressable past relations. For example, many in Mrs. Brookenham's circle believe, correctly at first, that Longdon is trying to recover Lady Julia through Nanda. Disturbing the present by forcefully recovering the past would deny Nanda an original self; and in fact, the "novel's closing portrayal of the retreat of Nanda Brookenham and Mr. Longdon to the ahistorical realm of Beccles suggests their inability to separate past from present, to recognize their possibilities as inhabitants" of the present.[16] Meanwhile, Mrs. Brookenham's fear that she will be displaced by her daughter in the circle of courting gentlemen, is a fear of premature succession (perhaps a contributing factor to monstrous, apparently uncontrollable growth). She feels that she is losing effect—again, losing authorial control—and that Nanda's authorial powers and effective charms will intervene and supersede

16. Mizruchi, *Power of Historical Knowledge*, 69.

her own. That Vanderbank, like the adored reader, is considered a desirable partner for both mother and daughter reinforces the confusion of past and present. And Longdon's attempt to make his memory of Mrs. Brookenham's mother contiguous to her daughter leaves Mrs. Brookenham herself outside the diptych frame of his vision of succession.

Similarly, the Duchess's close watch over Aggie's innocence assures that Aggie will not become part of the drawing room circle; to use James's prefatory, horticultural analogy, the Duchess sees to it that Aggie cannot flower naturally, and thus cannot displace her guardian. The threat of natural generational succession causes those who stand to lose most to intentionally prevent the process from progressing. Mrs. Brookenham suppresses Nanda by keeping her outside the drawing room; the Duchess intervenes between Aggie and the world, keeping Aggie all potential, and inadvertently inciting others to try to author her story. When Nanda enters the drawing room circle, Mrs. Brookenham's "readers" (her gentlemen callers) do not know which figure to attend to. And when the overripe but still green Aggie finally enters into normal social relations her latent sexuality is exceedingly pungent. Intentions are confused all around as would-be narrative subjects begin vying in the foreground for the attentions of their readers, usually unaware of the would-be authors who seek to subsume them in their narratives.

Nanda's initial absence from the circle makes her, like Aggie, an extremely attractive authorial property. The process of Nanda's development from child to young woman was hidden by her mother. Nanda's "reality" was suppressed and in its place all sorts of narratives could reside. In the preface James indicates that Nanda is like the historical seed that threatens to appear to the attentive reader. Her recovery so thoroughly complicates the aesthetic structure created by her mother that the unified "smooth general case" presented by Mrs. Brookenham "is really all the while bristling and crumbling into fierce particular ones" (9:xi). James forewarns us that "Nanda's retarded, but eventually none the less real, incorporation [into her mother's circle] means virtually Nanda's exposure" (9:xi): the threat of incompletion that James perceives in the appearance of the originating seed becomes in the narrative the threat of displacement.

Nanda turns out to be a powerful authorial presence who aggressively resists, as Vanderbank does passively, being subsumed by others' narratives but who, unlike Vanderbank, authors narratives that involve others and herself. The failure of any single author to wrest complete authority over the narratives of his or her subjects results in authorial anarchy, and this is precisely what James fears will result from naming the historical origin of *The Awkward Age*: alternate narratives will rival his own and bleed power from it. He is not threatened by the actual seed or germ, but by the authorial designs of others upon that original impression. The threat is intentionally stayed in the preface by making the threat itself the suppressor of the threatening agent: the threat of confrontation with origins induces the author to produce fully grown (in fact, overgrown) product, whose forceful presence displaces its own past.

Alternate narratives are feared by both sisters, Mrs. Brookenham and the Duchess, because both are insecure in their authority. As Nanda and Aggie come of age, they not only threaten to be their elders' rivals within the fading sisters' world, but worse, to break away and create independent aesthetics in which neither adult has any authority or control of meaning. The problem, however, is not their actual displacement, but the strategies they develop to cope with the threat of displacement. James sets an example of the appropriate response in the preface, where he displaces the history of the book's development with a recounting of various compositional choices he made. James relates alternate plots, contexts, literary models, typographical presentations, and rewards for success. He goes so far as to describe what he calls the *idée-mère*—the general notion (or narrative structure) that may take any number of dramatic turns and result in countless variations—from which the crafted product eventually evolves. The cultivating consciousness must choose along the way the specific process of germination and hence control narrative growth. Yet although James can describe the choices he made and the alternatives he shunned, he does not describe—in fact, he claims to forget—how the narrative grew into the substantial novel that it is. In this sense, James (ironically) echoes Marx: while men make history, they do not know that they are making it. According to the preface of *The Awkward Age*, James was making crucial decisions about composition while being ignorant of the overall narrative structure to which these decisions were contributing. The model offered in the preface, however, argues that one must make difficult, often controversial decisions that are true to one's standards, and that one must own up to them. Only then may one assume the rights of authorship.

Mrs. Brookenham denies her choices and so inadvertently undermines her own authority. She claims that Nanda is not kept out of the drawing room specifically to prevent premature succession of gentlemen's attentions from mother to daughter; therefore she has no adequate defense against demands that Nanda be produced. Longdon, on the other hand, always has his alternatives before him. He could attempt to mold Nanda (unsuccessfully) into a replica of Lady Julia; he could court Nanda for her own virtues; or he could try to marry her off to a gentleman of his choosing. He can make his choice only by acknowledging (at least to himself) his motives. That Nanda herself might claim so forcefully the power to choose is an element of the subject Longdon is eventually treating.

In the preface James, unlike Mrs. Brookenham and her sister, advocates choice and challenge, citing the result as the true indication of authorial power; however, that power seems undermined by James's contention that narrative growth was in fact out of his control. He recalls his initial intention to write a short work, then he points embarrassingly at the narrative's considerable length. James implies that authorial choices are powerful properties; each choice opens views to new narrative worlds that might not have been apparent prior to that choice. Desirable complications of plot and subtleties of character may be invisible during the early stages, and remain so if the author chooses incorrectly. James creates the illusion that choices are still possible, as if the text were still being composed. While the acts of electing choices are not always remembered, the choices elected are inscribed in the narrative: they are, in effect, the narrative that the author reads. By recognizing his "participation in the flow of past events," James acknowledges "responsibility for their outcome, which is not merely a privilege but a necessity" for James if he is to assume authority over the narrative that results.[17] James recognizes what Mrs. Brookenham does not, that acceptance of competition and acceptance of the past afford greater control over both. In addition, the reader experiences vicarious empowerment as he or she is meticulously led through the maze of compositional management; and, if he or she accepts James's suppositions on which compositional choices were made, the reader is induced to feel partially responsible for (and proud of) the outcome as well.

James's inability to recover so many of the choices he has made, and his production of hypothetical alternatives to those choices he has recalled, indicate that he is far less concerned with accurate historical narrative than with shoring the text against the straining of the critical reader who might come (in particular to the New York Edition) untutored in James's style. By offering the reader the same alternatives he might have considered, James gives the reader the vicarious experience of authorship, of being James himself. James assumes that the choices that he made—even if the act of

17. Mizruchi, *Power of Historical Knowledge*, 67.

choosing is itself a forgotten event—will be endorsed in spite of any criticisms leveled against them. The representation of criticism of James's choices, in fact, replicates the decision-making process by reproducing the conflicting voices from which James had to chose his course of action. Invented criticism is for James in the prefaces always a set-up for inventing both history (what would have been said) and authority (choice and recollection of choice). In effect, James asserts that he, and not the critic, has the power to cultivate both the narrative (with "consequent authority") and the reader.

In both *The Aspern Papers* and *The Awkward Age* unsuccessful attempts at authorial control result in narrative anarchy: no would-be authors have control of the origins of his or her narrative, and so none had real authority over it. The Aspern scholar, unlike Longdon, confused the past with his desires for control over the past; as a result he failed to produce anything but a pseudohistorical narrative of his own failure. And even in this instance, the scholar, now the narrator, is dependent to an unspecified degree on an external object for his authority and identity: the tiny portrait of Jeffrey Aspern. Longdon, on the other hand, separated his history of Lady Julia and his authorial desires for Nanda. He is the retiring but successful author figure, whose historical knowledge and authorial abilities provide a frame in which Nanda can exist free of suppression by her mother and possession by a husband.

James does not always suppress history, as he does in the preface to *The Awkward Age*, or appropriate it as he does in the preface to *The Aspern Papers*. Dramatizations of the scenes of origin and of writing often displace the naming of the origins themselves, or subsume them into the frame narrative of the author in the act of creation. James frequently follows these tales of composition with discussions of particular scenes from the narrative, thereby allowing the reader to preview actions that will be read later, in the critical context provided by the preface. Such previsions of the narrative create another sort of history. When the reader encounters these scenes in the narrative, she will bring to her reading a foreknowledge of them, with preconceptions carefully manipulated by the author, who hopes to fulfill his own desires for an ideal reader by shaping the reader's first experiences of the text.

4

AUTHORIAL PERFORMANCE AND SUBVERSIONS OF READING

The Wings of the Dove and *What Maisie Knew*

Once James establishes his voice in the prefaces as the sonorous voice of truth—the voice of the creator and the privileged reader of the text—he begins to create through instruction and his own example the ideal reader of his work. This reader is, of course, James himself. And the prefaces afford James a podium from which he may speak eloquently and convincingly about his novels and tales without interjecting his critical voice into those texts and thereby destroying the illusion of the fictive world. James could use the prefaces to interpret each of his novels, but such practice would be uncharacteristically tactless for James; it would demystify his art. He is not concerned with telling us what the fiction means; instead, he explains how well it is crafted. And again, he is not so concerned about showing us his craft as he is determined to teach us how to read attentively and thereby to appreciate his artisty. He employs several strategies to accomplish this. Two selected from the eighteen prefaces will serve, I hope, to demonstrate James's critical approaches to his work and most important, to the reader. The preface to *The Wings of the Dove* presents a heroic struggle with the bifurcated consciousness of that text. James claims that he is not completely satisfied with the outcome, but in the process he positions himself in the place of his noble and sacrificial heroine, Milly Theale, and elicits sympathy, perhaps even empathy from the reader. *What Maisie Knew*, on the other hand, offered James an equally difficult challenge, and he explains carefully in the preface that he has succeeded in delimiting the central consciousness in this novel to the mind of a young girl who must convey through the narrative far more worldly knowledge than she can possibly articulate to us or to herself. Both strategies of self-criticism and self-praise are attempts by James to prepare the reader for the novels that follow, and to keep the reader attentive to James's authorial performance.

In *The Rhetoric of Fiction*, Wayne Booth argues that James "objected most strenuously" to " direct appeals to the reader's moods and emotions" because they "call the reader's attention explicitly to the fact that he is reading just a story."[1] Such demystification of the novel is clearly seen by Booth, and by James, as a diminishing, perhaps even demoralizing, experience for the reader. Booth is referring specifically to self-praise by the author that interrupts the story's narration, yet he continues to push his case beyond qualification: "Any kind of praise of one's work for its artistry implies, it might seem, a lack of reality in the world with which one's artistry deals. And certainly any direct self-praise by the author, however wittily disguised, is likely to suggest that he can do as he will with his characters." In fact, Booth prefaces *The Rhetoric of Fiction* by arguing that Henry James makes specific rhetorical moves in an "effort to help the reader grasp the work," and that Booth himself is "pursuing the author's means of controlling his reader."[2] Yet for Henry James, praise of his own work and occasional criticism are the main strategies by which he attempts to control consumption—both reading and appreciation—of his art. To maintain the integrity of the fictive world while calling attention to his artistry, James relegated self-praise and other forms of criticism to the prefaces, framing his fiction with what so many of his readers have since considered the most appropriate tools with which to construct critical discourse about it. By framing his work in prefaces that repeatedly and painstakingly refer to the artistry and performance that the novels and tales manifest, James seems determined to force his reader to attend "explicitly to the fact that he is reading" not "*just* a story," but nothing other than a story—an exquisite aesthetic edifice.

Referring to authorial performance, the prefaces transform the prefaced novels and tales into self-conscious artworks through the "prefaced" reader's informed consciousness. James makes this abundantly clear in the preface to *The Turn of the Screw*, a novel that is, James says in the preface, both a fairy tale and an "exhibition": it is both story and literary performance.

---

1. Wayne Booth, *The Rhetoric of Fiction* (Chicago: University of Chicago Press, 1961), 205.
2. Booth, preface to *The Rhetoric of Fiction*, n.p.

Just as the reader must become engaged in the desperate plight of the Governess who would save her charges from "the haunting pair" of ghosts who are "capable, as the phrase is, of everything—that is, of exerting, in respect to the children, the very worst action small victims so conditioned might be conceived as subject to"—the reader is to witness another equally compelling drama, that of the author "allowing the imagination absolute freedom of hand, of inviting it to act on a perfectly clear field, with no 'outside' control involved, no pattern of the usual or the true or the terrible 'pleasant' (save always of course the high pleasantry of one's very form) to consort with" (12:xvi). James compares himself as author to the Harley Street employer of the Governess, who, like James's imagination, is granted supreme authority at Bly. That is, James seems to abdicate authority on the one hand only to snatch it with the other: his realistic, historical sense delegates authority to his imagination, whose performance we will witness, just as we read and evaluate the performances of the Governess (as Governess, as narrator, as author). James intends our evaluation of his work to be far less equivocal than our consideration of the Governess. This attention to authorial performance results in what Stephen Donadio considers a "sustained dramatic irony" between the author and "even the most lucid of his characters" because "the author is able to maintain at all times his superiority." The text, Donadio says, becomes a "demonstration" of the author's superiority, which derives from the "author's comprehensive awareness," which "serves as the larger frame within which the account of the more or less unsuccessful efforts of individual characters to unravel the tangle of their lives is finally placed." By limiting the purview of his narrative to a central reflective consciousness—and this is a main tenet of James's aesthetic of fiction—James implicitly reminds us of "an unattainable ideal of total clarity" that would present "a view of *all* the dimensions." Yet this comprehensive view, Donadio says, "has been attained at least by the author, who remains in precise control," but who cannot exercise his power to clarify what the central consciousness leaves a blur.[3] Just as the Harley Street uncle of Flora and Miles demonstrates his despotic power by exercising his ability to delegate it, James seems to cede control of the origin and development of *The Turn of the Screw* to his seemingly disembodied imagination, and implicitly therefore recalls his own absolute authority over the text.

3. Stephen Donadio, *Nietzsche, Henry James, and the Artistic Will* (New York: Oxford University Press, 1978), 149–50.

The terms James uses to discuss authorial performance vary widely in the prefaces. He refers to it as sacrifice and religion in one preface, while in another he sees himself involved in playful sport. The range of metaphor in the prefaces suggests, according to Laurence Holland, that "'calm' and order of the kinds which characterize most earlier literary theory . . . are as absent from the essays as is the belligerency of controversy—that the strength as well as the tenor of the essays derives rather from the euphoria and anxieties of James's intimate involvement with his fiction. . . . The Prefaces . . . dwell on the paradoxical interconnection of masterly success and artistic failure. And it is the torment (the profound doubts as well as the satisfactions) of these encounters, and the articulated pressures behind them, that give the essays their force."[4] This force, the essential drama of authorship, is turned on the reader, sometimes in an effort to reason with, and other times in an attempt to coerce, the reader to envision the text as it would be in the author's ideal reconstruction of it even when the text reveals authorial failure (as is the case with *The Wings of the Dove*, according to James). The author is most heroic, however, when he is confronting the greatest difficulties occasioned by his adherence to an aesthetic of fiction that depends upon the illusion of an autonomous central consciousness; therefore James is most heroic, and most dramatic, in his authorial performance of *What Maisie Knew*, which he considers a resounding triumph.

Having established his authority over writing through the historicizing tales of origin, James begins to wield his power over reading. Yet the author, as Corneille suggests, must not interfere in the prefaced narrative, though that would be the easiest way and most convenient place to instruct the reader. Still, the author must somehow interfere in the reading. Corneille admonishes the author to remain in the margins, augmenting the text carefully. James agrees, but he uses the marginalized frame to guide the reader to a greater appreciation of the artistry of the text, not to indicate ancillary actions and ideas or to demonstrate that his comprehension is superior to that of the central characters. Nor is his goal to induce the reader's appreciation of the novels and tales. The discussion of critical method and authorial performance in the prefaces demonstrates the author's superiority *as an author*, and the demonstration is rehearsed to convert the reader to a nearly worshipful appreciation of the author's profound aesthetic capabilities.

4. Laurence Holland, *Expense of Vision: Essays on the Craft of Henry James* (Baltimore: Johns Hopkins University Press, 1964), 155–56.

The preface to *The Wings of the Dove* shows James with great ambition as the author and with equally great uncertainty as reader about his success. James carefully directs our attention to the compositional challenges that he faced, always explaining the theory that guided his endeavors, and then questions whether or not the book "reduces itself to a just notation of the law" that he earlier articulates (19:xii). The drama of *The Wings of the Dove* would hinge on "a young person so devoted and exposed, a creature with her security hanging so by a hair," and who therefore could not "but fall somehow into some abysmal trap." Yet the drama itself is only part of the text: "a great part of the interest [would] also reside in the appearance that she would constitute for others," most especially Kate Croy and Merton Densher (19:ix). James set out to locate his narrative in more than one consciousness; each lucid reflector would take his place temporarily at the center of the fictive world from which he would register the narrative world, the main object in which is the heiress Milly Theale. The trick, James contends, was to fix the reflecting centers "so exactly that the portions of the subject commanded by them as by happy points of view, and accordingly treated from them, would constitute, so to speak, sufficiently solid *blocks* of wrought material squared to the sharp edge, as to have weight and mass and carrying power; to make for construction, that is, to conduce to effect and to provide for beauty" (19:xii). The image of James as mason was first introduced in the third preface, in which he talks about his relationship to his reader being a matter of carefully laying brick upon brick; he extends it here in order to focus on craft, precision, and magnitude: "The building up of Kate Croy's consciousness to the capacity for the load little by little to be laid on it was, by way of example, to have been a matter of as many hundred close-packed bricks as there are actually poor dozens" (19:xiv). This is the image with which James presents his successes, which are always solid and exact.

Yet the preface to *The Wings of the Dove* is not a salutation to James's realized method; it is a careful delineation of what has been realized and what has not, of what was intended and what has occurred. His failures are pictured in perhaps greater detail, but in images of less substance. Densher's "final position and fullest consciousness," for example, "was to have been marked in fine stitches, all silk and gold, all pink and silver, that have had to remain, alas, but entwined upon the reel" (19:xv). Reducing Densher's consciousness to adornment, James is able to evaluate his novel favorably in spite of its deviation from his intention; according to this metaphor, Densher's consciousness never was to be part of the veritable structure of the novel. Its absence, therefore, may well be missed only if James's intentions are articulated, and therefore we might wonder why James brings this up at all. One reason might be that the failure to realize his intention to include a section that is focalized through Merton Densher is not a sign of James's inability but of the restrictions of form: fullest presentation of Densher's consciousness "was to have to come to us in a deeper draught out of a larger cup" (19:xv). James could not begin to fit all that he wanted to write into the already extravagantly long novel, which was threatening to grow all out of proportion to its natural shape and length (we might recall the "monstrous" growth of *The Awkward Age* in this regard). And the form, James then implies, is dictated to a great extent by circumstances that are inseparably aesthetic and pragmatic.

And thus we return to the discussion with which James begins his explanation of intention and method in *The Wings of the Dove*. After explaining just how precarious a subject Milly Theale is, and that she would be the structural "key" at the center of the narrative, James notes what might be taken as his failure to keep her in focus. Strangely, he couches this admission in terms of authorial freedom and comfort rather than of failure. "From the moment I had comfortably laid the ground provided in my first Book," James says, "I felt" that the "metal *did* hand free . . . [and] the free hand, in this connexion, was above all agreeable" (19:xi). Yet in the first book, Milly is "superficially so absent"; James became infatuated instead with Kate Croy's voluptuous consciousness. And he luxuriated in it: "I scarce remember perhaps a case—I like even with this public grossness to insist on it—in which the curiosity of 'beginning far back,' as far back as possible, and even of going, to the same tune, far 'behind,' that is behind the face of the subject, was to assert itself with less scruple." The conciousness of Kate Croy, in other words, fascinated James to such an extent that he dwelled on (in) it at length, perhaps for too long, before employing it to the intentions with which it was created. These failures to realize intention, though born of freedom are eventually attributed to James's nemesis, the literary marketplace: "the freedom . . . I owed to the fact that the work had ignominiously failed, in advance, of all power to see itself 'serialised'" (19:xi). James's luxuriant prolonging of the first book of the novel, and his delayed introduction of Milly Theale, are responses to the novel's initial failure on the literary market. James was never forced to write from the very beginning with proportion and volume in mind. This sudden freedom from the strictures of serialization, he notes, at first allowed him to explore the deep subtleties of one aspect of his aesthetic, but it ultimately disallowed the completion of another: Densher's consciousness is never developed and, though occasionally superimposed on Kate's, it is never distinct. The blame falls, he claims, on the "world of periodicals and editors, of roaring 'successes' in fine, amid which [the novel] was well-nigh unnotedly to lose itself." "There is fortunately something bracing," James then says, "ever, in the alpine chill, that of some high icy *arête*, shed by the cold editorial shoulder" (19:xii). Although the " 'conditions of publication' " are "conceived in a light liable to represent *within* the circle of the work itself little else than darkness," they explain the compositional choices James made when faced with the unbridled freedom born of utter rejection. Given the opportunity to write without deadline or some concrete compositional goal, James elected to go behind, to go further back, to probe Kate Croy's consciousness more and more deeply, rather than to move forward. This is another manifestation of the preference he reveals in the frame: to read beneath the text, to unearth the origins of the text and of himself as its creator. The admission, moreover, is not threatening to James because he knows that in the last preface he will demonstrate the successful performance of the dual consciousness.

Certainly James could have attempted to justify the compositional choices he made as he does; for instance, in the preface to *The Awkward Age* where he rehearses authorial performance by citing several major compositional problems, the alternative solutions that were present to him, and the choices he eventually made. He elects instead to discuss in finer detail than we can find anywhere else in his oeuvre the Jamesian aesthetic of fiction; this discussion is punctuated by the sometimes frank admissions that *The Wings of the Dove* is hardly a perfect example of that aesthetic (James confesses his "scarce more than half-dissimulated despair at the inveterate displacement of the general centre" and names the novel "the most striking example . . . of my regular failure to keep the appointed halves of my whole equal" [19:xviii]). Yet between this periodic self-criticism (the causes for which, we should remember, are attributable to the crass realities of the profession of authorship), James elaborately describes the successes of the novel— successes, by implication of his excessive freedom, that can be attributed to nothing and to no one but the author himself:

> I note how, again and again, I go but a little way with the direct— that is with the straight exhibition of Milly; it resorts for relief, this process, whenever it can, to some kinder, some merciful indirection: all as if to approach her circuitously, deal with her at second hand, as an unspotted princess is ever dealt with; the pressure all round her kept easy for her, the sounds, the movements regulated, the forms

and ambiguities made charming. All of which proceeds, obviously, from her painter's tenderness of imagination about her. (19:xxii)

The result of his careful and highly evaluative analysis in the preface to *The Wings of the Dove* depends entirely, of course, upon the reader. If James's guidance does not find a receptive reader, as the preliminary plan for *The Wings of the Dove* apparently did not, then James's work in the preface is for naught. Yet James, like Marlowe in Conrad's *Lord Jim*, who contends that "those who do not feel do not count,"[5] directs his remarks to the reader already indoctrinated (either by prescience or by the previous fifteen prefaces and seventeen volumes of the New York Edition):

> (Attention of perusal, I thus confess by the way, is what I at every point, as well as here, absolutely invoke and take for granted; a truth I avail myself of this occasion to note once for all—in the interest of that variety of ideal reigning, I gather, in the connexion. The enjoyment of a work of art, the acceptance of an irresistible illusion, constituting, to my sense, our highest experience of "luxury," the luxury is not greatest, by my consequent measure, when the work asks for as little attention as possible. . . .) (19:xx–xxi)

We are reminded that James as author reigns over the text, and that he is meticulously explaining how that text is to be understood and appreciated. We are also reminded that as readers, we have very great responsibility if we are to demand great pleasure.

Sometimes James's critical discourse leaves a distinct track through the text for the reader to follow in order to *subvert* critical reading rather than to enable it. The preface to *What Maisie Knew* transforms the text into an example of James's method, but it also and perhaps more insistently attempts to coerce the reader into a judgment of the text, and of authorial performance, that might not otherwise be rendered. The "delightful difficulty" of writing *What Maisie Knew*, James says, is that the narrative would be centered in the consciousness of a young, naive girl. She will be his lucid reflector, sometimes reflecting elements of a world that she does not fully understand. Unlike George Eliot's Maggie Tulliver, for example, who enjoys the benefit of a reflective narrator, Maisie alone will create an impression of her world, if we

---

5. Joseph Conrad, *Lord Jim* (New York: Penguin, 1961), 166.

are to believe the rhetoric of the preface. As the title implies, her awareness is both the agent and the object of James's novel. Whereas the preface to *The Wings of the Dove* implies that James was exploring the boundlessness of his subject's consciousness, the preface to *What Maisie Knew* focuses on the limits of consciousness. James claims in the preface to be a silent partner in the business of representation, but he fears that, should he leave his central consciousness to her own devices, the novel will prove that what Maisie knew is insufficient for the reader, and the reader will have no choice but to consider James a failure at this difficult aesthetic challenge.

Rather than compromise his aesthetic principles completely or risk the reader's disapprobation, James attempts to subvert the reading of *What Maisie Knew* through the discourse of the preface by repeatedly asserting that his authorial performance is a success. James presents his challenge in this way: as author, he must navigate the rough waters between obtrusiveness and the supposed transparency of realist narration. To achieve a "systematic surface . . . beyond reproach," the author, not Maisie, "should have to stretch the matter to what [she, as] wondering witness materially and inevitably *saw*" but had no capacity to comprehend without revealing himself like an overzealous stage parent who enters the spotlight and thereby destroys the illusion of the autonomous performer (11:ix). Presumably, to be caught by the reader in the act of supplementation would be to compromise the integrity of his aesthetic, and so of himself. His narrator, however, is not under such constrictions, and so James can supplement Maisie's consciousness through the aegis of the narrator. The narrator is distinguished from the author in that he is actively engaged in the immediate and ongoing construction of Maisie's narrative, whereas the author, identified throughout as Henry James, and given voice only in the preface, is the conscious creator of both narrator and Maisie. The structure of *What Maisie Knew* further distinguishes these agents. The author speaks in the preface; the narrator speaks sotto voce in the prologue; the narrator articulates Maisie's consciousness in the prefaced, prologued narrative that follows. Yet even the narrator must be restrained; otherwise he threatens to be unmasked as the guiding, fretting author himself. Ideally, and as the preface predicts, *Maisie*'s narrator will articulate what Maisie has no vocabulary to intellectualize without usurping her role as framer of the narrative world.

In most of James's work, the role of the narrator is not so problematic; most adult reflectors in James's fiction have a great capacity for self-awareness that is contingent upon equally great comprehension of the world. Lambert Strether of *The Ambassadors* is a fine example; the story culminates when he "at all events *sees.*" This "process of vision," James confides proudly, reflects on the author: it is "the business of my tale and the march of my action, not to say the precious moral of everything" (21:vi). *The Portrait of a Lady*'s Isabel Archer is another protagonist with an expansive consciousness. During her famous night vigil, Isabel determines her fate based on her suddenly profound understanding of the situation and circumstances into which she has fallen. In these novels, the narrator is meant to be a vehicle (James uses the metaphor of a carriage) with which the central, reflecting consciousness transports his or her fictive world to the reader. Six-year-old Maisie, on the other hand, as James well understood, "would at best leave great gaps and voids" in the composition that reflects, and is a reflection of, her consciousness (11:ix). These gaps, James contends, would result from the child's limited lexicon, not her immaturity. Children "have many more perceptions than they have terms to translate them; their vision is at any moment much richer, their apprehension even constantly stronger, than their prompt, their at all producible vocabulary" (11:x). The narrator's task in this case is to supplement the child's limited vocabulary with "commentary [that] constantly attends and amplifies" but that does not overreach her precocity (11:x). The narrator and Maisie will collaborate: he will couple his words with her emotions. Yet in spite of what James says in the preface, when Maisie's emotions and impressions are inarticulate, the narrator must violate her consciousness, imposing vocabulary that comprehends what she perhaps does not. His goal in these instances is to produce a narrative that is borne of the union of her consciousness and his commentary, and that takes her as its subjective object.[6] In the preface, however, James claims to have succeeded from beginning to end of the novel at making the narrative a perfect collaboration of narrator and Maisie. Yet the two scenes that James selects with which to demonstrate his success are arguably the only two scenes in the novel in which narrator and Maisie collaborate so symbiotically.

In the first stage of her narrative, Maisie's awareness of her new circumstances in life grows fitfully, often as the result of parental battle. James initially focuses narrative on Maisie rather than through her, showing how

---

6. Merla Wolk argues that the narrator's task is "like that of the mother who structures and interprets the otherwise chaotic world of the very small child." But Wolk believes all that James says in the preface, that the narrator augments Maisie's world, allowing her (and the reader) to understand it but stepping aside as soon as Maisie is old enough and wise enough to render her own world articulately. Thus Wolk denies James's subversion of Maisie's narrative authority. "Narration and Nurture in *What Maisie Knew,*" *Henry James Review* 4 (Spring 1983), 196–206.

Maisie acts rather than telling what she knows, because in the beginning Maisie comprehends very little. But as Maisie becomes self-reflective, James portrays both her actions and her feelings, for Maisie's reflections proffer the reader's view of her world. Yet Maisie often seems void of the emotions most expected of a child in her situation, and frequently, the narrator articulates Maisie's unexpressed feelings in order to allay the reader's suspicions that Maisie is being forced to feel more than she could possibly understand. For instance, staying longer than the legally allotted six months with her father and her governess, Miss Overmore, "she got used to the idea that her mother, for some reason, was in no hurry to reinstate her" (11:35); seemingly abandoned by her mother, Maisie calmly resigns herself to her fate.[7] But these are the narrator's words, not Maisie's. Clearly she has no vocabulary to comprehend her feelings, nor has she the experience to fully understand what it is, in fact, that she does feel about her abandonment. Narrative "commentary" supplements its portrait of Maisie, inferring a direct relationship between how Maisie appears and what Maisie feels. The narrator reads and interprets Maisie, and this suggests that the author does not trust the reader to interpret for him- or herself. Rather than show Maisie peacefully enjoying the seventh, eighth, and ninth month of her six-month tenure with Beale Farange, the narrator intrudes to explain what he apparently fears will not be revealed by plot or scene, or if it is revealed, will be misunderstood by the reader.

At key moments throughout the novel, however, the narrator emerges, reminding the reader that Maisie is being assisted. For example, while strolling in the park Maisie and her stepfather, Sir Claude, unexpectedly encounter her mother with a strange escort, the Captain. Shortly thereafter Maisie and her stepmother, Mrs. Beale, unexpectedly discover Mr. Farange with an equally strange attendant. In both instances the stepparents had believed their spouses were abroad. Both parents had lied and both had been found out through their indiscretions. After Maisie's second encounter with parental indiscretion, the narrator interrupts to point out that the unidentified "sense" of the situation that Maisie had was "something that in

---

7. James has been criticized for not exploring the moral and emotional abuses perpetrated on his child protagonist. As many critics have noted, Maisie's lack of reactions make her parents' misdeeds seem less cruel. Perhaps this is precisely what Maisie is up to. She is denying what she cannot fully understand, but she cannot suppress what she feels. The critical debate focuses on Maisie's innocence. See, for example, Oscar Cargill, *The Novels of Henry James* (New York: Macmillan, 1961), 244–62.

a maturer mind would be called the way history repeats itself" (11:172). The narrator not only articulates what Maisie feels, which James calls the "passion that precedes knowledge" (11:xiv), he relates her feeling to the process of maturation that results from the history that is peculiarly her own—the history of parental (and stepparental) immorality and indiscretion, yet a history that she has not yet lived through. For this brief moment, the narrator glimpses the entire picture of Maisie's life, and subtly suggests the quality of Maisie's eventual retrospections. Nevertheless, the narrator admittedly reaches beyond Maisie's comprehension in this aside to the reader, placing Maisie within a frame outside of which the narrator and reader stand. By interpreting Maisie's unidentified sense, the narrator prepares the reader as James has done in the preface. He replaces the child's lack of experience with the reader's greater understanding and knowledge, and thus implicates the reader in his subversions of the supreme authority of Maisie's subjective consciousness. Yet the narrator in this instance is not interpreting Maisie's actions; he is articulating what, he says, she clearly feels but for which she has no words.

More dramatically, at a crucial later moment, the narrator interjects a long explicative passage as a corrective to Maisie's very mistaken interpretations of her stepfather's actions. After Maisie has been utterly abandoned by her biological parents, she is left in the dubious custody of her stepparents, Sir Claude and Mrs. Beale, who are romantically involved. The one voice of rigid morality is Maisie's maternal governess, Mrs. Wix. All along Mrs. Wix's moral apprehensions have supplemented Maisie's intuitions, especially on the subject of Mrs. Beale's relations with Sir Claude. Furthermore, Mrs. Wix has argued persistently for a domestic arrangement among Sir Claude, Maisie, and herself. Thus when Sir Claude *without* Mrs. Beale takes Maisie to the southern shore of England and on to France, Maisie believes that soon she, Sir Claude, and Mrs. Wix will establish a peaceful, settled household without Maisie's stepmother. Maisie thinks she for once will be loved and cared for because of who she is, not what she signifies to the world. Sir Claude seems greatly heroic to Maisie at this moment. Yet the narrator plainly contradicts his temporarily less-than-lucid reflector:

> It was granted her [Maisie] at this time to arrive at divinations so
> ample that I shall have no room for the goal if I attempt to trace the
> stages; as to which therefore I must be content to say that the fullest
> expression we may give to Sir Claude's conduct is a poor and pale
> copy of the picture it presented to his young friend. Abruptly, that

morning, he had yielded to the action of the idea pumped into him for weeks by Mrs. Wix on lines of approach that she had been capable of the extraordinary art of preserving from entanglement in the fine network of his relations with Mrs. Beale. The breath of her sincerity, blowing without a break, had puffed him up to the flight by which, in the degree I have indicated, Maisie too was carried off her feet. (11:202–3)

While Maisie has read Sir Claude's intentions correctly, she has misread his courage and determination. The narrator thoroughly undermines the independence of the subjective consciousness, yet he couches this subversion in words that nearly glorify Maisie's intuition. The narrative's unusually objective view of circumstances and motivations draws on an intricate weaving of diverse registers of diction, beginning with "it was granted her . . . to arrive at divinations," which seems to revert to the style of the prologue in which Maisie's consciousness is never entered into.[8] In fact, through the narrator, James is holding Maisie at a distance, making her the object of his narration.

The violation of Maisie's autonomy by her narrator, like the violation of her trust by Sir Claude, indicates the restrictions of Maisie's sovereignty and the limits of her consciousness. The narrator could have let stand Maisie's mistaken, romantic vision of her stepfather so that the reader might then experience more fully the force of Maisie's disillusionment when Sir Claude surrenders to his tragic weaknesses. The narrator, in fact, could be utterly mindless vocabulary, nothing more than narrative mediation. He is not. The narrator subverts Maisie's impression of Sir Claude with a more accurate representation, and this is ironically called a pale imitation of the false original. We are subtly reminded that Maisie is only a child, who sometimes displaces probability with dreams, and also that Maisie's dreams constitute the greatest good (they are more humane, for example, than Mrs. Wix's stale Victorian morality).

8. In her chapter on *What Maisie Knew*, Carron Kaston notes the satiric use of Latinate and legal diction in the prologue, and argues that this generalizes the description of Ida and Beale Farange's scandalous, vindictive proceedings as a sad but typical melodrama. See *Imagination and Desire in the Novels of Henry James* (New Brunswick: Rutgers University Press, 1987). If it generalizes the plot, the diction makes the story a social commentary. The preface suggests as much when it relates the social type from which Maisie was ultimately drawn. Stripped of the subjective consciousness it would supplement, the prologue is the bald articulation of Maisie's situation without reference or deference to her subjective consciousness of it.

In this passage James exercises his authority over his subject by having the narrator correct Maisie's misperceptions. James thereby reminds the reader that this is his performance, not Maisie's. However, to diminish the disturbance that such direct vision of Maisie's world creates, the narrator portrays Sir Claude in terms of what Maisie thinks she knows. Literally, we see the poor, pale, but true copy before we encounter the false original. James rescues the reader from the child's delusions, yet maintains focus on the child's capacity for awareness by delineating this overstepped limit. The narrator then sounds a roundly satirical note: the true genesis of Sir Claude's doomed efforts to be heroic was the "breath" of Mrs. Wix's "sincerity, blowing without a break": it "had puffed him." Maisie may imagine the ideal, but Mrs. Wix, with not altogether selfless motives, coaxes Sir Claude to reach beyond his capability. Thus both adults, and Mrs. Beale as well, are implicated in the eventual shattering of Maisie's dream, but the narrator decidedly is not. This is not an example of James's parental guidance of his young charge; it is a theft of the powers of the subjectivity with which he endowed her. If Mrs. Wix persuades Sir Claude to act with greater moral vision than he actually possesses, James does not force Maisie to comprehend more than can reasonably be expected. He allows the narrator to step outside Maisie, to look at her and to evaluate her vision rather than contort that vision to conform to a precocity that even Maisie could not maintain. James compromises his reliance on the subject's consciousness as the center of the fictive world rather than risk the appearance of flawed authorial performance.

As if to accommodate this breach of his aesthetic, James has the narrator promise two things: (1) that Maisie's misunderstanding is the result of several states of "divination" (a mixture of passion and induction); and (2) the existence of a narrative "goal" that is not adversely contingent on Maisie's misinterpretations. The goal is presented as the narrator's, not Maisie's, and as this passage well demonstrates, the truth of vision is also the narrator's, even when it contradicts Maisie's reflections of her world. When Maisie momentarily fails as the lucid reflector, she is replaced by the more reliable narrator, but only until the crisis of false reflection is passed. A valued standard of truthful representation, it seems, must be maintained in this collaboration, toward which Maisie contributes as much as she is able. The narrator makes up the difference. This passage suggests that the degree of the narrator's presence is at any moment the measure of what Maisie does not know. Conversely, the absence of narrative intrusion indicates the approaching plenitude of Maisie's comprehension.

The narrator is not always so compulsive about identifying what Maisie herself can not analyze, or about correcting what Maisie has misapprehended. When at the end of chapter 5 Maisie imagines that her doll Lisette was cross-examining her as to her whereabouts, Maisie replied, the narrator explains, "as she, Maisie, had once been replied to by Mrs. Farange: 'Find out for yourself.' " The narrator interprets: "she mimicked her mother's sharpness, but she was rather ashamed afterwards, though as to whether of the sharpness or of the mimicry was not quite clear" (11:34). Maisie does not yet interpret what she experiences, except as her experiences are registered emotionally. In this instance the narrator is satisfied with ambiguity. He does not feel compelled to delineate Maisie's motivations. He violates her less and trusts the reader more.

Both Maisie's history and the narration of her history culminate not when Sir Claude sends Maisie off with Mrs. Wix, but when what Maisie knows is the wonder of Mrs. Wix and, more important, the wonder of the narrator: the profound truth of her circumstances as it is reflected in her fully accurate understanding of Sir Claude. In fact, Maisie seemingly moves beyond the narrator's ken at this point. Toward the end, when Mrs. Beale's desire for Sir Claude allows her to believe that anything is possible "with a little diplomacy and patience," the narrator responds, "I may not even answer for it that Maisie was not aware of how, in this, Mrs. Beale failed to share of his [Sir Claude's] insurmountable distaste for their allowing their little charge to breathe the air of their gross irregularity" (11:205). The narrator seems to imply that he does not have a full account of what Maisie does and does not know. Moreover, the narrator next turns directly to the reader and exclaims, "Oh decidedly I shall never get you to believe the number of things she saw and the number of secrets she discovered!" (11:205). Maisie unsettles the narrator's moral and aesthetic authority. Whereas before the narrator betrayed the falsity of Maisie's intuitions in order to reach his author's goal, here the narrator simply gives up his role as articulator. Sometimes, then, the narrator's abilities to articulate, just like Maisie's to understand (or at least to see passively), are not up to the mark. Like the overabundance of material, this void threatens to undermine the narrator's authority. The reader must somehow grasp that Maisie comprehends far more than she seems capable of, that she intuits knowledge almost magically, it seems, and yet is prone to misunderstand, particularly when she acknowledges her own capacity to desire. Maisie's introspective reflections do not exclude the narrator; the narrator's inability rests in his relationship with his reader. He situates himself, though helplessly, between the reader and Maisie, acknowledging his responsibility. Though he laments the impossibility of portraying the completeness of Maisie's understanding, he in fact frames Maisie as the subject of his author's portrait of her.

All of James's prefatory discussion of the narrator's role implicates the author as the ultimate dramatic subject of the ideal reading of this text, which becomes the history of James's struggle with the delightful difficulties of so difficult a subject. The Jamesian reader is asked to attend to the plane of determination in which Maisie, the narrator, Sir Claude, Mrs. Wix, and all the others are compositional components of the author's aesthetic creation. Our attention is directed to the unified smooth surface, the finished artwork that signifies the author's power and ability. From this perspective, James can justify his compromise of Maisie's autonomy: supplementing her consciousness is not a sign of weakness in the original design but rather a blatant subversion of meaning by method. As the preface suggests, what the story is about matters less than how the story means. How narration represents the narrative world supersedes the narrative world represented.

In fact, the essential elements of the story are foretold in the preface, directing the reader away from plot and toward authorial performance. James's first accomplishment was his choice of subject. James loses himself, he says, in the appreciation of his young *ficelle*'s ability to transform the vulgarities of her plot into "the stuff of poetry and tragedy and art" (11:xii): the narrative's primary concern, in other words, is not to relate the story of Maisie, but to relate the construction of an artwork. Yet poetry and tragedy and (literary) art are articulations, requiring vocabulary that comprehends "the stuff": articulation, however, is precisely the skill that James has already said Maisie has not adequately developed. Articulation through the narrator is unmasked as another crucial aspect of James's authorial performance. However, articulation alone leaves the variously ignoble adults in Maisie's world "too poor for conversion [to the stuff of art], of too short a radiation, too stupid . . . , too vain, too thin" to warrant—to deserve—being the subjects of a literary composition; Maisie's presence among them creates aesthetic value just as her presence among the adulterous couples fosters the illusion of their moral value. She aesthetically redeems her family's society by making her relatives and their associates "*appreciable*," James says (11:xii). And this value is what the narration seeks in its articulations. Like the narrator, James will collaborate with Maisie: James requires Maisie to increase the value of his composition; Maisie needs James, he says, to articulate her world.

By offering an outline of the story and presenting specific scenes as pre-texts to the author's criticism in the preface, James disables plot in order to enable positive evaluative interpretation of his art. The preface to *What Maisie Knew* pre-views the narrative to force it into a frame of repetition in which the prefaced narrative is experienced by the reader as a duplicate of the idealized reading in the preface. J. Hillis Miller refers to this mode of repetition as Platonic: it asserts that the repetition's identity and value devolve from its similarity to the original. This mode of repetition valorizes the preface because, in the course of reading, the preface and the authorial consciousness that informs it are encountered first. The preface seeks to assure that the reading of the narrative will repeat James's reading of his own work, whether it is accurate or not, in order to subjugate the reader as a Platonic repetition, one who is identified by his or her likeness to the original—the author.[9]

In fact, James has doubly framed *Maisie* with summaries of its plot: the prologue, like the preface, predicts that Maisie's fate is to be "a ready vessel for bitterness, a deep little porcelain cup in which biting acids could be mixed" (11:5). Like the certain destiny that these summaries compel, the framing visions of her future remain completely outside Maisie. She is no more and no less than one of the several contested items in her parents' divorce settlement. Thus the preface and prologue complicitly distinguish James's possession of Maisie from her parents' possession of her. Her parents will violate by negating her needs and replacing them with their own desires; James, through his narrator, will violate by supplementing her consciousness with commentary. Yet what James uncovers in the preface he re-covers with the prologue's ironic and detached tone. James shows his reader what the story would be like if he were to perform it without Maisie. Moreover, the prologue allows James to show Maisie's parents as Maisie, at so young an age and as yet so uninvolved with their hatred of each other, cannot: as self-absorbed and sadly comic. For example, Ida Farange is described in the prologue as "a person who, when she was out—and she was always out—produced everywhere a sense of having been seen often, the sense indeed of a kind of abuse of visibility, so that it would have been, in the usual places, rather vulgar to wonder at her" (11:7–8). Beale Farange is equally visible. He has "natural decorations, a kind of costume in his vast fair beard, burnished

---

9. J. Hillis Miller, *Fiction and Repetition: Seven English Novels* (Cambridge: Harvard University Press, 1982).

like a gold breastplate, and in the eternal glitter of the teeth that his long moustache had been trained not to hide and that gave him, in every possible situation, the look of the joy of life" (11:8). These are portraits of the parents without the child, fittingly drawn in the only section of the narrative in which the child's consciousness does not participate.

In his effort to idealize reading (and the reader), James identifies two scenes near the middle of the novel that demonstrate what he considers ideal collaboration between narrator and Maisie. These scenes represent moments in narrative during which Maisie and the narrator are so closely connected that, at times, what Maisie sees and experiences, and the articulation of her vision and experience, coalesce in what appear as instants of the child's enlightenment but that are more accurately the narrator's capacity to duplicate the child's consciousness and comment on the situation she perceives. James selects these scenes partly because they are the moments when an idealized reading will most likely occur; in them Maisie becomes articulately aware of what had been before only felt by her as a "passion that precedes knowledge." What Maisie sees blends with what Maisie knows; her roles as subjective consciousness and narrative object overlap; and Maisie's reflections of her world and James's narration of those reflections converge.

The first scene of collaboration that James brings to the foreground in the preface is Maisie's meeting with her father and the strange dark woman, Mrs. Cuddon, with whom Maisie's father is about to travel to America. "The facts involved," James says by way of setting his discussion in context of the plot, "are that Beale Farange is ignoble, that the friend to whom he introduces his daughter is deplorable, and that from the commerce of the two, *as* the two merely, we would fain avert our heads" (11:xii). Plot is reduced to the essentially moral qualities of its elements, which are always of great concern in James's work, and the absence of redemptive circumstances nearly disqualifies this scene as acceptable to James's aesthetic sensibilities. "Yet the thing has but to become a part of the child's bewilderment for these small sterilities to drop from it and for the *scene* to emerge and prevail" (11:xii). James depends upon Maisie just as Mrs. Beale does, to recompose immorality into a scene that holds Maisie in its focus and so is redeemed with social significance (for Mrs. Beale) or aesthetic significance (for James). Thus both use Maisie as a frame that crops reality and makes it a semiotic field. Yet Maisie alone is not enough: for the scene to "prevail" it must be "vivid, special, hard wrought, to the hardness of the unforgettable" (11:xii). Added to Maisie's mediating reflections are James's authorial powers. If Maisie's bewilderment redeems the tawdry subject, James effects an aesthetic apotheosis of authorial performance.

Initially, Maisie feels as if she is in a fairy tale: as she leaves the exhibition with her father, the "pitch of the wondrous was in everything" (11:177). James prefers to restrain his narrator, keeping him from violating Maisie's consciousness in order to point out the irony of her emotions, except perhaps in the most subtle way. Her father's meager kindnesses, his "vague affectionate helpless pointless 'Dear old girl, dear little daughter,' " affected Maisie's imagination so forcefully that "it needed nothing more than this to make up to her in fact for [her father's] omissions" (11:180). James prefers to allow his young subject's intuition to remain in control even though it threatens to misinterpret Beale Farange's motives. Yet in this scene Maisie's consciousness is profound. As Beale Farange continues to seduce his daughter's admiration, Maisie intuits his real motives for being kind.

> She was conscious enough that her face indeed could n't please him if it showed any sign—just as she hoped it did n't—of her sharp impression of what he now really wanted to do. Was n't he trying to turn the tables on her, embarrass her somehow into admitting that what would really suit her little book would be, after doing so much for good manners, to leave her wholly at liberty to arrange for herself? (11:186)

Realizing that her father's invitation to join him in America is in fact his way of unburdening himself of the responsibility of caring for her, Maisie rises to his expectations and hopes, sets him free with a helpless murmur, " 'Oh papa—oh papa!' " (11:187). While the adults in Maisie's life continually fall short of her expectations for them, she continually manages to meet their demands. Maisie "understood as well as if he had spoken it that what he wanted . . . was that she should let him off with all the honours—with all the appearance of virtue and sacrifice on his side" (11:187). Maisie hears the unspoken, and the narrator, instead of translating Maisie's feelings into overcomprehending discourse, expands narration to discover the full extent of Maisie's knowledge. "It was exactly as if he had broken out to her: 'I say, you little booby, help me to be irreproachable, to be noble, and yet to have none of the beastly bore of it. There's only impropriety enough for one of us; so *you* must take it all. *Repudiate* your dear old daddy—in the fact, mind you, of his tender supplications. He can't be rough with you—it is n't in his nature: therefore you'll have successfully chucked him because he was too generous to be as firm with you, poor man, as was, after all, his duty' " (11:187). Since Maisie is too innocent and too kindhearted to have the words with which to describe her father's motives, the narrator must invent narration—in this case, dialogue—to explain what Maisie intuitively knew.

This dialogue is not presented by James as supplementation; it is a representation of *how* Maisie knew her father's intent. Unlike in the beginning of the novel, in this scene the narrator does not supplement Maisie's consciousness by explaining what she does not understand. The narrator supplements the narrative in order to supplement the reader: James wants the reader to feel what Maisie feels: to do so, the reader must see in one moment what Maisie has seen and experienced her entire life—Beale Farange at his deceptive and charming best. Thus the assumed plenitude that appears lacking is not Maisie, for she understands full well what is going on. It is not the narrative, for it shows the paternal abandonment and the child's duplicitous reaction. What the author fears may be lacking is the reader. The frame of *What Maisie Knew* provides experience to the reader of Maisie's narrative world, of the artwork that contains it, and of the authorial consciousness that creates and consumes it. The frame alters what is framed, but more important, it alters what is outside the frame by conditioning it— the reader—to the artwork and to the narrative world within as the author would have the reader experience them.

The second scene that James pre-views in the preface concludes his reconstruction of an ideal reader. Throughout her meeting with the dark lady and her father, Maisie is repeatedly reminded of her meeting in the park with the Captain, a strange but kind friend to her mother. This encounter James also brings to the foreground in the preface, and so he too must find deep narrative and emotional connections between the two events. Walking in the park with Sir Claude, Maisie is confused about the identity of her mother's companion. Her confusion is picked up by the narrator (as collaborator), who calls the brave-looking stranger "the Count" (Ida's previous suitor) as long as Maisie believes this to be his identity. When the encounter finally occurs, Maisie feels strangely absent as the others speak of her as the object she had long since become to them. Maisie shies away from the fiery anger of Sir Claude's rebuke to her mother, and retreats to a more pastoral park bench with the Captain—whose ambiguous identity seems acceptable to both Maisie and the narrator—and for the first time she sees, through the Captain, a vision of her mother that is entirely new, if unrealistic.

The Captain's endearing sketch of Ida as an angel, as a tremendously kind and loving woman who is "tremendously" fond of her daughter, but who thinks that Maisie does not like her, is as alien to Maisie as is Mrs.

Cuddon, but far more attractive to a child raised on her mother's rejection. The Captain's final, almost epiphanic assertion that Ida is "*true!*" brings Maisie a throb of joy,

> still less utterable than the essence of the Captain's admiration. She was fairly hushed with the sense that he spoke of her mother as she had never heard any one speak. It came over her as she sat silent that, after all, this admiration and this respect were quite new words, which took a distinction from the fact that nothing in the least resembling them in quality had on any occasion dropped from the lips of her father, of Mrs. Beale, of Sir Claude or even of Mrs. Wix. . . . so that at the touch of it something strange and deep and pitying surged up within her—a revelation that, practically and so far as she knew, her mother, apart from this, had only been disliked. (11:151)

The revelation forces Maisie to reconceive the past, as she realizes that "Mrs. Wix's original account of Sir Claude's affection seemed as empty now as the chorus in a children's game," suggesting that at this point Maisie has dropped her child's way of thinking (11:152).

At no point in this dialogue does the narrator intervene to remind the reader of Ida Farange's real character, nor does he articulate beyond Maisie's comprehension. The narrator reveals the passions that this encounter stirs in Maisie, but does not evaluate them from a perspective that is maturer or greater in any respect than Maisie's own. This scene demonstrates the range of Maisie's emotions and the capacity of her sensibilities not to idealize or romanticize, but to sympathize with someone she desperately wants to love, her mother. Rather than demand her own security, she demands some sort of security for her mother: "'Say you love her, Mr. Captain; say it, say it!' she implored" (11:153). Whereas in the scene with her father Maisie comprehends lucidly his baser motives that are left unspoken by him but articulated by the narrator, in this scene Maisie grasps the deep sadness and loneliness that embitters her mother, and wishes for her mother's sake that the Captain will offer Ida Farange some salvation.

In both scenes, the narrator leaves the force and substance of communication to Maisie, in her spoken words and in the description of her thoughts and feelings. The narrator and Maisie collaborate so closely here that neither is ever completely distinguishable. The artistry that James points out so emphatically is this transformation of a sordid meeting among three adulterers and a child: it becomes the illumination of the child's powerful compassionate nature and of her own peculiar emotional agenda. That Maisie is capable of such love is a wonder of her own being, and a wonder of James's aesthetic ability to carry it off so effectively. "The active, contributive close-circling wonder, as I have called it," James says, "in which the child's identity is guarded and preserved, and which makes her case remarkable exactly by the weight of the tax on it, provides distinction for her, provides vitality and variety, through the operation of the tax—which would have done comparatively little for us had n't it been monstrous" (xiv). In this scene, Maisie's identity is guarded first and foremost by narration that remains true to her perceptions and emotions, that does not articulate beyond her capabilities, and that does not objectify her.

These scenes are presented in the preface as exemplary but not unusual. James uses them to subvert reading of the rest of the text, hoping (a bit like Beale Farange) that the reader will see aesthetic valor that is not always there, and that the reader will react accordingly. All of these subversions of reading occur in the preface so that *What Maisie Knew* will signify what James accomplished (or what he would have his readers believe he accomplished). The preface boldly reveals the author as the deified creator of Maisie's narrative world. As he first sketches the story that he found as a wind-blown germ, James begins to handle it, to reshape it, to transform it. He considers the aesthetic dangers involved in his authorial performance in the narrative; as he does so, James becomes engaged once again in the challenge. The "glimmer became intense" as he proceeded "to a further analysis" of the germ, refining it until he "was in presence of the red dramatic spark that glowed at the core of [his] vision and that, as [he] blew upon it, burned higher and clearer" (11:vi). Recalling the moment when the seed of a narrative was internalized in the "light of . . . imagination," James changes his tone. He does not speak satirically, as he did when first considering the story of "some luckless child" who would be treated like a "tennis-ball or shuttlecock" that rebounds from "racquet to racquet," or from parent to parent (11:v). Nor is his subject held at a distance; she is meticulously examined as the authorial property that will demonstrate James's craft of fiction, and though still referred to as "the child" rather than as "Maisie," the subject is quickly embroiled in all of the narrative circumstances from which Maisie emerges. Since the preface is the product of retrospective reading, this prefatory re-production of Maisie is an illusion that recalls the association of creation and creator. Maisie is shown as the child of her author's imagination. As she becomes more fully realized in the preface through James's recollection of her development, Maisie

increasingly signifies James's power as her author. And the story, too, is the
child of its author. In no other preface does James so forcefully demand that
the prefaced narrative be understood as a systematically constructed work
of art, of which he is the architect and master builder.[10]

The critical apparatus in the prefaces works on the sensibilities of the
attentive reader, teaching her James's aesthetic and then introducing the
prefaced text as that aesthetic objectified. This being the case, the prefaces
contribute to what Fredric Jameson claims is the "critical revolution" of
formalism: they constitute a "radical inversion of the priorities of the work
of art" because they force the reader "to suspend the commonsense view of
the work of art as *mimesis* (i.e. possessing content)."[11] In place of mimesis,
James's art becomes performance. The prefaces to *The Wings of the Dove*
and *What Maisie Knew* invoke the great challenges of authorship in the
age of what is presented as anti-aestheticism in the marketplace. They ask
the reader to appreciate the novels for the accomplishment that they are,
and also for the intended accomplishments that they now gesture toward
thanks to the critical narratives that frame them. The prefaces transform the
prefaced narratives, in other words, by interfering with them, and with the
reader, and with the world that both text and reader inhabit. As Stephen
Donadio claims, the author assumes a position of superiority to all three—
the text, the reader, the world—because ultimately he would have all three
act as signifiers of his supreme authority.[12] The text becomes a history of
his struggles to compose; the reader reads for authorial performance; the
imperfect text signifies an imperfect world and an idealized author who
therefore does not fit in that world except as totem.

10. In the preface to *The Portrait of a Lady,* in contrast to this preface, James seems to disown
the narrative, to attribute it to delegates who are nevertheless distinctly other. See Chapter 6.

11. Fredric Jameson, *The Prison-House of Language: A Critical Account of Structuralism and
Russian Formalism* (Princeton: Princeton University Press, 1972), 82–83.

12. Donadio, *Nietzsche, Henry James, and the Artistic Will,* 110–18.

5

Meaning, Context, Intertext

A Preface to Ten Tales

Of the New York Edition's twenty-four volumes, nine contain more than one narrative. For each of these nine volumes James selected tales generally related by theme or subgenre. For example, tales of contrasting cultures are collected in volume 14 ("Lady Barbarina"), and volume 11 (*What Maisie Knew*) contains three narratives that explore points of view limited by age, experience, and physical boundary.[1] Relating the stories collected in one volume, James creates a compound semiotic field that encourages his reader to understand each story in relation to the principle informing its volume. That is, each multinarrative volume promotes a reading of the stories that understands them as intertexts that are in some meaningful relationship to one another, a relationship that is usually semiotic and formal, and occasionally (and arguably) practical (in terms of the exigencies of publishing). Intertextual reading crosses narrative borders. Yet while ideas, themes, symbols, and character types may be reinvented in several collected tales, the narratives that reinvent them are distinct and idiosyncratic. Like the multipanel picture frame, the bound volume itself might act as the constituting agent. The

---

1. On James's selection of tales for these volumes, see especially Edel, *Henry James: The Master: 1901–1916*, 321–30; Michael Anesko, *"Friction with the Market": Henry James and the Profession of Authorship* (Oxford: Oxford University Press, 1986), 141–62; and Edward Stone, "Edition Architecture and 'The Turn of the Screw,'" *Studies in Short Fiction* 13 (1976): 9–16.

preface offers a suggestion, an indication, sometimes even a dissimulation of James's intention to create intertextual meaning. The meaning is gleaned by the informed reader rather than received by the anxious author. Rather than point out the aesthetic success of his performance, as he does in the preface to *What Maisie Knew*, in the prefaces that encourage intertextual reading James employs a different strategy. He discusses both the practical and philosophical concerns of authorship and art in order to court if not virtually create the reader with a nature similar to his own. Through this strategy James attempts to frame the reader within "a geometry" that is peculiarly his own (1:vii), and thus to assure that reading will uncover and appreciate James's authorial performance. A brief history of the interpretation of *The Turn of the Screw* will demonstrate how successful James has been in coaxing his readers to attend to authorial performance, including his performance as architect of the New York Edition.

The most celebrated, and still mystifying case of interpretation-by-volume is the case of *The Turn of the Screw*. The significance of this tale's placement in volume 12 after *The Aspern Papers*, and before "The Liar" and "The Two Faces," has contributed to several "anti-apparitionist" interpretations of James's most enigmatic story, first and best championed by Edmund Wilson.[2] James has left a telltale clue, Wilson and his supporters contend, that indicates that the truth of the tale is revealed outside the text in the stories that physically bracket it. According to Wilson, *The Aspern Papers*, which is the first narrative in volume 12, is "a study of a curiosity which becomes a mania and menace," and the tale that follows *The Turn of the Screw*, "The Liar," is "the story of a pathological liar whose wife protects his lies against the world, behaving with the same sort of deceptive 'authority' as the governess in 'The Turn of the Screw.' "[3] Found in the company of maniacs and psychotics, the Governess herself must be the victim of delusions or James would have placed her story elsewhere. Wilson's argument is based on two assumptions about narratives as semiotic fields: there is a correlation between physical context and identity, and the borders separating these

2. On the relationship of James's placement of "The Turn of the Screw" in volume 12 and its interpretation, see especially Edmund Wilson, "The Ambiguity of Henry James," *Hound and Horn* 7 (1934); published in revised form in his *The Triple Thinkers* (New York: Oxford University Press, 1948), 90–95; Leon Edel, "The Architecture of Henry James's 'New York Edition,' " *New England Quarterly* 24 (1951): 169–78. For a rebuttal of these contextual arguments, see Edward Stone, "Edition Architecture and 'The Turn of the Screw,' " to whose work I owe much of my summary of the debate. "Anti-apparitionist" is Stone's term.
3. Wilson, "Ambiguity," 390; and *Triple Thinkers*, 94.

narrative semiotic fields must be violated to gain a critical perspective that is broad enough, in this case, to encompass the psychological context in which the Governess is best understood. In effect, Wilson comprehends meaning through a dialectic of inside and outside, then dismantles that dialectic without precluding it.[4]

Ever since Wilson's startling assertion that the Governess of Bly is mad as a hatter, critics who would like to counter Wilson's argument have been forced to consider why James didn't place *The Turn of the Screw* with the ghost stories in volume 17. Edward Stone's study of volume context has gone farthest to challenge Wilson's conclusions without negating his assumptions. He claims that the Edition's publisher required that the number of pages in each volume fall within a restricted range so that the volumes would all be approximately the same size. Stone contends that this restriction of James's editorial freedom dictated the placement of *The Turn of the Screw* in volume 12, disregarding the thematic similarity or disparity of the tales. While Stone acknowledges the existence of volume identity, he questions the efficacy of relying on it as an exigetic tool. He argues "if not [for] a theory of mere coincidence" of volume construction, at least for "the impression that the architecture of James's edition, as regards the central volumes (10–18), was either not precisely planned or not precisely executed."[5] Stone's argument accounts for the extraliterary pressure exerted on the creation of the New York Edition, but it does not address James's uncharacteristic prefatory silence on the subject of his placement of *The Turn of the Screw*. James mentions *The Turn of The Screw* in the preface to volume 17, in his discussion of the ghost story, but he never alludes to its [dis]placement in another volume. Yet discontinuity of relations among the stories in a volume is significant to James, enough so that he usually addresses the discontinuity in the preface. James explains at the outset of his discussion of "Julia Bride," for example, why he placed this relative of "poor little dim and archaic Daisy Miller," whose story begins volume 18, at the end of volume 17: "I have placed 'Julia Bride,' for material reasons, at the end of this Volume, quite out of her congruous company . . . ; and mainly with this drawback alone that any

4. Identifying the conceptual frame of volume 12 and enacting its work through an intertextual reading, in other words, might reveal that the pathology one finds in *The Aspern Papers* and "The Liar" spills over into *The Turn of the Screw*; by the same token, and though unconsidered by Wilson, Edel, and others, the ambiguity of *The Turn of the Screw* might cloud the clear diagnosis of pathology in those neighboring tales.

5. Stone, "Edition Architecture and 'The Turn of the Screw,' " 9, 16.

place of criticism she may seem formed to provide rather misses its link with the reflexions I have here been making" (17:xxv). Apparently, Stone does not assume that intention resides in James's silence—intention of placing the Governess among her own kind.

The evidence that Stone presents is persuasive enough to cast a shadow over Wilson's monumental interpretation; however, insofar as the *nature* of the evidence supporting his assertions, Stone apparently does not believe his own final conclusion that "the case for 'The Turn of the Screw' as a study in obsession rather than a ghost story must rest on . . . intrinsic . . . grounds": he bases almost one-third of his argument on other, extrinsic frames of reference—James's prefaces—gesturing dramatically toward the prefaces' role in forming volume identity.[6] He implies that one should look not only to the stories themselves to reveal the logic of a volume; one should examine the comments James makes in the multinarrative preface and consider the extraliterary circumstances of the marketplace in which the Edition was published. Like Wilson, then, Stone is ambivalent about the integrity of the border that distinguishes what is internal to the narrative and what is external. And, like Wilson, Stone expands the border into a frame of reference in which internal and external concerns are unified through the agency of the author's critical consciousness as he selects and edits the texts to be included and arranged in each volume. Wilson contends that that consciousness is primarily concerned with thematic unity; Stone claims that the practical concerns of publishing sometimes are paramount. Both arguments imply that the consciousness evident in the arrangement of each volume is given direct voice only in the preface. The preface provides the only authorized frame of reference through which James attempts to instigate and control intertextual reading. Although the contextual debate has never resolved itself in some rectifying reading of *The Turn of the Screw*, its most important contribution to the study of James's novels and tales in the New York Edition is the implication that a multinarrative volume has hermeneutical significance. A story's "truth" or "meaning" might be determined by considering its inclusion in a volume and its consequent relation with other stories in that volume because the narratives in a single volume fall within the bounds of a conceptual frame through which inter-textuality is enacted. The conceptual frame of a volume must be raised to the surface, therefore, and made visible; only then might a tale, though it

---

6. Stone, "Edition Architecture and 'The Turn of the Screw,' " 16.

can and has existed individually, be understood as part of the complex relation of interactive compositional elements that are arranged by the author within the volume. This last phrase is key: the reader must attend to the author's logic of arrangement, not necessarily to the stories themselves. Again, authorial performance is brought to the fore as the central concern of the New York Edition and so of James's ideal reader.

James makes his most protracted statements about volume context and identity in the preface to volume 17, which includes "The Altar of the Dead," "The Beast in the Jungle," "The Birthplace," and many of his ghost stories. These ten tales are brought within one frame of reference to meet James's expressed desire to uncover the common elements of the tales and his unarticulated desire to suppress other determining relations, especially origins and histories of writing, which he claims repeatedly to have forgotten. Unlike the preface to the stories concerning the life of the artist, this preface does not overtly identify a common theme; however, it explains rather elliptically that the tales fall into three "range[s] of representation," in each one of which the author explores "the subject of his own wondering" (17:xvii). James says that in each range of representation, the author's "prime care has been to master those [subjects] most congruous with his own faculty . . . or in other words to the production of the interest appealing most (by its kind) to himself" (17:xvi). The ranges of representation, in other words, reflect James's aesthetic appreciation of and affinity for particular subjects; in this way, they signify his identity as a writer.

The purpose of his construction of a self-reflective volume of tales, however, is not self-gratification. The tales are brought together here, James writes, in the hope, "with all achievable adroitness, of causing [the reader] to wonder" at the same concerns (17:xvii). The reader of this volume, in other words, will gradually model his or her behavior after the author's and thereby become totemically identified with the author. This frame is an expression of James's "desire, amid these collocations, to place, so far as possible, like with like"—story with story, *ideal reader with author*—in a union that would validate, and increase the value of, the author's aesthetic vision (17:ix). The conceptual frame of this volume, then, seems to be the gradual union of the dialectically opposed author and reader, self and other. During the course of the volume, however, the dialectic will take many forms.

These comments suggest that James will employ a framing strategy that begins by identifying the various subjects of his wondering and then demonstrate how those subjects are mastered by being subjected to his aesthetic of fiction. We are to understand, however, that these subjects and the tales in which they are inscribed, gesture toward the master himself, whose "faculty" is the standard by which they have been judged. And James has not entirely misled us, yet the subjects of his wondering are not only the subjects taken up in the tales, but also the tales themselves as aesthetic objects with economic value. The first range of representation is framed by several expressions of James's frustration at the apparent disparity between the great intrinsic, aesthetic value he perceives in his own works—a value he hopes his readers will also perceive—and the extrinsic value of those works as commodities. Each narrative's history as a commodity is so disturbing to James that the tales of origin repeatedly devolve to each narrative's failure on the marketplace. " 'The Altar of the Dead,' " James begins the preface, "forms part of a volume bearing the title of 'Terminations,' which appeared in 1895. . . . I have to add that with this fact . . . and the fact that, as I remember, it had vainly been 'hawked about,' knocking, in the world of magazines, at half a dozen editorial doors impenetrably closed to it, I shall have exhausted my fund of allusion to the influences attending its birth" (17:v). The "accidental determinant" of the "The Beast in the Jungle," though "of comparatively recent date and destined, like its predecessor, first to see the light in a volume of miscellanies ('The Better Sort,' 1903)" is lost: James confesses, "I remount the stream of time, all enquiringly, but . . . come back empty-handed" (17:ix). The origin of "The Birthplace" is quickly recalled, but recast as a brief summary of the story's narrative situation. James offers no other situation or circumstance of his reception of the germ, only the germ itself. Having essentially summarized the conflict in the tale, he dispenses with further discussion of "The Birthplace" and takes up the fantastic tales that follow.

By suppressing the origins of the first three tales and replacing them with their publishing histories, and then using these histories to establish a framework in which James introduces the thematic concerns of the stories, James constructs a bridge between the realms of art (image) and world (reality) that Wilson and Stone have constructed dialectically. In *Aesthetic Theory*, Theodor Adorno has argued that art must oppose, or attempt to negate, the exterior world and, as part of that world, its own anterior existence. Art seeks "blissfully or unhappily, to seclude itself from the world" in order to establish semiotic integrity: "it is by virtue of its separation from empirical reality that the work of art can become a being of a higher order, fashioning the relation between the whole and its parts in accordance with its own needs." Yet the dialectic of art and the world, and art's desire for utter seclusion, constantly remind us of the relation of art and the world it would obfuscate, as James understood. Adorno claims that this relation continues in the face of art's attempted negation of the world because the dialectic of art and reality derives from the social dialectic in which art is "both an autonomous entity and a social fact in the Durkheimian sense of the term." Art is both a product and a record of production: it is viewed extrinsically as a commodity and it views itself (or is viewed) intrinsically; therefore, as James laments, the work must be doubly evaluated.[7]

The dialectic of art and reality, where reality is understood as the social fact of the production process, is promoted by James in this preface as he negates the historical reality of narrative origin and generation, replacing it with an assumption of narrative presence. The tales of origin begin here, that is, with the stories already written and ready for publication. Yet by framing the tales with their economic histories, James has fully incited extraliterary (real) discourse: he may negate the notion of the stories as compositional process, but he reifies their narrative worlds as economic products. Displacement of narrative origins by discussions of commercial history initially brings into focus the real value of James's art as products of the culture industry. James does not, however, place extrinsic, economic and intrinsic, aesthetic values in dialectical opposition as Adorno does, particularly as Adorno allies these poles with the dialectic of the profane and the sacred; James is lamenting the disparity of these values and suggesting an ideal parity for which he strives.[8] In this preface James seeks a relation between extrinsic value, which registers in the realm of reality (the realm of objects, signs, histories, commodities, and contexts), and intrinsic value, which registers in the realm of what Hans Robert Jauss calls irreality (the realm of meaning, signifieds, aesthetics, and atemporal, noncontextual existence—the transcendent realm of Art).[9] What Adorno would have as the autonomous realm of Art, and would experience aesthetically and intellectually only, James acknowledges is at least penultimately material and real, particularly in the form of the printed text that confronts the reader. And although James expresses his desire

7. Theodor Adorno, *Aesthetic Theory*, trans. C. Lenhardt (London: Routledge and Kegan Paul, 1984), 6–8.

8. Adorno does claim that "even the most sublime work of art takes up a definite position *vis-à-vis* reality," but Adorno insists that this position must be polar and oppositional: the work of art steps "outside of reality's spell, not abstractly once and for all, but occasionally and in concrete ways, when it unconsciously and tacitly polemicizes against the condition of society at a particular point in time" (*Aesthetic Theory*, 7).

9. Hans Robert Jauss, *Aesthetic Experience and Literary Hermeneutics*, trans. Michael Shaw (Minneapolis: University of Minnesota Press, 1982), 13.

to have his works considered for their intrinsic, aesthetic qualities rather than as products of a culture industry with nonaesthetic (or anti-aesthetic) standards, he freely and repeatedly admits that the tales themselves are commodities as well as works of art, and have apparently indelible histories as such. The New York Edition is nothing if not James's most elaborate and expensive product, and it is his most elaborate attempt to create a market for his art.

James effects a relation of reality and irreality in the preface by first constructing a relation of work and text. The preface calls the reader's attention to both the extrinsic value and the intrinsic value of the narratives; and although these values are not equivalencies, they are interactive and they suggest interaction between the two realms they represent. In fact, all three "ranges of representation" are concerned with this interaction of reality and irreality, represented variously as economics and aesthetics, relative and absolute truth/identity, physical and metaphysical reality, present and past existences. This becomes the conceptual framework that adheres the tales into a compound semiotic field that, as the preface predicts, itself signifies the author's consciousness and his desire for an ideal reader. Practically speaking, the conceptual framework fosters an intertextual reading of the tales in order to effect this signification.

In the First Range of Representation: An Intertextual Reading of "The Altar of the Dead," "The Beast in the Jungle," and "The Birthplace"

Two of the three tales least successful as commodities, "The Altar of the Dead" and "The Beast in the Jungle," are represented as the two most similar in the volume they are chosen to head and entitle (in addition to "The Birthplace," the least successful, and the third and final tale in this section). Their protagonists, George Stransom and John Marcher, are "fit indeed to mate" (17:ix), James says. In fact, the two tales tell much the same story; "The Beast in the Jungle" reinvents crucial formal and thematic aspects of "The Altar of the Dead"—they represent alike the author's concerns, both aesthetic and economic. In both tales "poor sensitive gentlemen" who have no material worries or apparent understanding of such, and who confront the world with a purist aestheticism that obscures physical reality, are coupled with women who, at least initially, have very real and practical concerns for their material welfare and whose broader perspectives include understanding of aesthetic vision and the pragmatics of necessity. In fact, these two stories and "The Birthplace" consider and reconsider the clash between the realities of economic necessity and the luxury of performing the strange devotions to irreality (conceived in sacred terms as the dead, the future, the unknowable past) that the protagonists believe are transcendent truths. Through the preface, James suggests a reading of these tales that confronts the frequent disparity between intrinsic and extrinsic value as this disparity is experienced by the man who is devoted exclusively to the intrinsic as a response to his confrontation with the commodity fetishism of contemporary society.[10] The preface articulates this aspect of the conceptual frame by implicating James and his text in the bind that variously characterizes the protagonists of the first three stories.

James explains that the work of art is always both real and irreal—commodity and image—and has its origin in both historic and aesthetic realms. Contrary to Adorno's belief, the artist consummates union between the real and irreal, because art is both semiotic (as text) and material (as work). To attribute value to only one of these qualities is to be consumed by either purist aestheticism or commodity fetishism, which, the tales reveal, are two faces of the same self-consuming beast. James explains that the confrontation of these extremes result in Stransom's cult of the dead:

> Frankly, I can but gather, the desire, at last of the acutest, to give an example and represent an instance of some such practised communion [with the dead], was a foredoomed consequence of life, year after year, amid the densest and most materialised aggregation of men upon earth, the society most wedded by all its conditions to the immediate and the finite. More exactly speaking, it was impossible for any critic or "creator" at all worth his wage not, as a matter of course, again and again to ask himself what may not become of individual sensibility, of the faculty and the fibre itself, when everything makes against the indulgence of it save as a conscious, and indeed highly emphasised, dead loss. (17:vi)

10. Such a confrontation is the polemical occasion for Adorno's aesthetic of negativity, Jauss claims (*Aesthetic Experience and Literary Hermeneutics*, 15).

When the world is consumed by the desire to consume, the "poor sensitive gentlemen" who are unable to create or at least to enter into a critical dialogue between the real and the irreal must turn in the real world to the worship of absence—the veneration of dead loss—represented by its image, for communion with a truth that is higher (that is, therefore, aesthetically purer) than economic necessity (17:ix). Yet James is careful to extricate himself categorically (as "'creator'") from the midst of these poor sensitive gentlemen. James desires to prove himself worth his wage (the wage he feels owed to him rather than the wage he has received), and so to conduct himself as a participant in the culture industry and as its critic. This balancing act between the real and the irreal liberates James from subservient devotion to either realm, the sorry fates of Stransom and Marcher.

In spite of James's "attested predilection" and embarrassing fondness for these "poor sensitive gentlemen," the reading instigated by the preface exposes Stransom's and Marcher's devotions to their immanent visions of truth as the ultimate, bourgeoise materialism—transformation of the Other (the women who befriend them) into utilitarian objects useful to their expressions of purist aestheticism. These "poor, sensitive gentlemen" commodify the women who love them, and employ these women in their idiosyncratic aesthetic industries. Similarly, in "The Birthplace" Morris Gedge thoughtlessly threatens his wife's emotional and economic security by worshiping that which he believes is signified only by fact—and therefore he venerates fact—as the antidote to the baseness of the culture industry that, he feels, has compromised his honor. Again, James distinguishes himself: he has paid unceasing attention to the needs of his Other—his reader—a concern he asserts repeatedly throughout the prefaces.

Stransom, Marcher, and Gedge fail to comprehend the importance of interrelating the self and other, just as they fail to appreciate equally the values of the real and the irreal. Stransom fails to appreciate the value of the love he might have in the present because he is consumed by his ritualistic observance of the dead, a practice that contains and valorizes his power and identity. John Marcher might enjoy his own love of May Bartram if he would only turn away from his observance of the future—which, like Stransom's observance, is in fact observance of the self.[11] And Morris Gedge is so terribly

11. Eve Kosofsky Sedgwick argues that Marcher's not-so-deeply submerged desire is not his ritualistic observance of the future, but rather what is named throughout the story by a series of preteritions—names that refuse to name. These preteritions are all common and characteristic labels, Sedgwick claims, for homosexual desire. Marcher's passion is not for May Bartram, even if his desire is *to desire* her. Although Sedgwick's argument is historically persuasive, it ultimately

consumed by historical truth and therefore by his relation to reality, that he fails to recognize the beauty and artfulness of his performance at the birthplace; to be satisfied with his performance would suggest satisfaction with his life (and wife).

Each failure takes place in, and attempts to negate the authority of the real, material world while expressing a desire for that world. The unrecognized truths are in each instance set in the context of the protagonist's failure to understand and appreciate the real, the concrete, the pragmatic and sensual necessities of everyday life, for example. In fact, all three "poor, sensitive gentlemen" are consumed by their strange observances that offer escape from those sometimes harsh or at least aesthetically poor realities. Stransom, for example, has no understanding of his fellow mourner's career and its remuneration. He understands her financial status in terms of the awkwardness it creates: at first, a gift from him might be understood as charity, but once she inherits a "tiny fortune" (17:33), he can rest easy: she has no need of his gifts and therefore he may freely give them or not, as his own desire dictates. Marcher has an even dimmer understanding of May Bartram's financial circumstances. That she is always at his side when he needs her is the greatest truth of her existence as he perceives it. Morris Gedge is temporarily perhaps the most dense of the three because he does not appreciate the loss both he and his wife would suffer should they lose their positions as caretakers of the famous poet's birthplace. His devotion to verifiable fact would destroy their economic and emotional security, yet he can think only of the absence of fact in his presentations to paying visitors. Isabel Gedge must carry the burden of worrying about their survival, which her husband jeopardizes by his disdain for what his employer calls "the Show" (17:188)—the performance of legend in lieu of the recitation of fact. Equivocal compromises between devotion to the irreal and acceptance of the real end the first two tales, but at the end of the third James presents a resolution that more closely resembles his own view of

---

seeks to reconstruct the text by naming what the text refuses to name, as she herself asserts. By attempting to force names that refuse to name yield their meaning—by attempting to force them to name, in other words—one demands substitutions, signs of signs. The sought-after, substitute signs signify the replaced preterition; thus Sedgwick, it seems, comes up with names that name names that refuse to name. What Sedgwick refers to as Marcher's homosexual desire, therefore, is her preferred name of what Marcher calls the beast in the jungle. See "The Beast in the Closet: James and the Writing of Homosexual Panic," in *Sex, Politics, and Science in the Nineteenth-Century Novel*, ed. Ruth Bernard Yeazell (Baltimore: Johns Hopkins University Press, 1986), 148–86.

the author as creator of aesthetic goods that have contingent extrinsic and intrinsic values.

Overtly the preface blames the commodity fetishism of society for Stransom's, Marcher's, and Gedge's predicaments, just as James must have blamed the culture industry for the poor reception of his works (especially of the New York Edition's first volumes, already in print when James was working on this preface). But James's endorsement of Stransom's and Marcher's intrinsic frames of reference is purposefully deceiving. As the preface otherwise indicates and as "The Birthplace" makes clear, James was working to bring the intrinsic and the extrinsic, the irreal and the real, the aesthetic and the material, into relations of equivalence. A more detailed reading of the first three tales will bring this process to light.

The first story in this range of representation is "The Altar of the Dead." The history of disparate aesthetic and economic values that James tells in his prefatory remarks about it seems ironic in light of the history of Stransom's alter as related in the story. At the opening of "The Altar of the Dead," George Stransom's life is "ruled by a pale ghost, . . . ordered by a sovereign presence": the dead loss of his betrothed, Mary Antrim (17:3–4). Rather than grieve passively and inwardly, Stransom creates a cult of the dead, and worships at an altar he erects on which one after another of his deceased friends and acquaintances are represented by burning candles. Stransom's devotion to the sacred at this point reflects James's insistence on the aesthetic. Yet the notion for Stransom's altar of brilliant light that makes the absence of his friends and acquaintances into a strange, illuminating presence comes to Stransom not from the similar though far more modest, traditional devotions of other mourners, but, the narrator explains, from the "particular effect of a shop-front that lighted the dull brown air with its mercenary grin and before which several persons were gathered. It was the window of a jeweler whose diamonds and sapphires seemed to laugh, in the flashes like high notes of sound, with the mere joy of knowing how much more they were 'worth' than most of the dingy pedestrians staring at them from the other side of the pane" (17:7). The sight brought to Stransom a strange vision of consumerist intercourse with his beloved: "Stransom lingered long enough to suspend, in a vision, a string of pearls about the neck of Mary Antrim" (17:7). This conflation of religious sentiment (the idea for Stransom's altar) and intimacy (Stransom's physical contact with Antrim) is thoroughly inculcated in Stransom as economically valorized power that he derives from economic disparity (the gemstones in the shopwindow are more valuable economically than the people admiring them, yet Stransom has the imaginative, and undoubtedly the financial, power to possess the jewels and to manipulate them as signs of his ownership of Mary Antrim). Moreover, the image he creates to express the extent of his loss is a sign of Mary's value: her neck is worthier of adornment than the shabby onlookers are worthy of the many necessities that might be purchased by an item of such great extrinsic value. The image implies that Stransom shares his materialistic imagination with at least the segment of society from which his economic status separates him most. The gems are not only unattainable, they contrast dramatically with the brown-stained world on the other side of the window, the world to which these people belong, the world in which Stransom so poorly fits. Unlike *The Princess Casamassima*, in which James presents a protracted vision of industrial society, "Altar" offers only this brief glimpse of the underbelly of capitalism, and does so in order to establish Stransom as an economically empowered misfit who is able to devote himself to the realm of the sacred not because he has no interest in the profane world of commerce, but because he is among that world's most privileged inhabitants. The image firmly grounds Stransom in his age by establishing the connection between his reverential behavior and, according to James in the preface to volume 17, the plague of his time: commodity fetishism.

The flashes of brilliant light reflected by the gems speak to Stransom of the joy of social superiority, which Stransom rightly conceives in economic terms. One might have expected Stransom to learn from his great loss that people are not to be commodified and assigned relative material value, but like Mortimer Scrooge he first must be shown what more he stands to lose. Stransom has made loss itself so precious that no one living could have nearly the value of any sign of the one (initially, and eventually, the many) who is (or are) dead. Thus like a clever broker, Stransom has transformed loss into enrichment, and he demonstrates the materiality of this transformation by seeing his altar of the dead revealed in his image of Mary's pearl-encircled neck.

When James takes up the subject of art as commodity in his prefatory discussion of "Beast in the Jungle," he does not create the same high degree of social and economic context that characterizes his discussion of "Altar," but he encourages a reading of "Beast" using "Altar" as a pre-text. The narrative's origin is lost, but its publishing history is recalled: it was "destined, like its predecessor ["Altar"], first to see the light in a volume of miscellanies ('The Better Sort,' 1903)" (17:ix). James's desire "to place . . . like with like" invites " 'The Beast in the Jungle' to stand here next in order" (17:ix). The stories are alike, James almost immediately explains, in that the

protagonists are nearly identical (17:ix). The expression of desire to mate
the stories (and their protagonists) precludes the tale of origin, and thereby
asserts forcefully that aesthetic relations in this volume take precedence over
historical fact. (This assertion foreshadows the resolution offered at the end
of "The Birthplace.") As James placed the tales together in the volume,
intrinsic, thematic concerns took precedence over extrinsic, historical, and
economic concerns, even though the tales' economic histories are similar.

Yet material concerns enter this section of the preface through James's
rhetoric: when James uses language in the preface that would involve Marcher in the world consumed by a desire for consumption, that language always
reveals shadows of absence and loss. James says that Marcher's "unrea-
soned prevision of some extraordinary fate" begins at "the threshold of his
career"—at a time in Marcher's life when he would otherwise be concerned
with success in the marketplace (17:ix). As a result of this prevision, Marcher
is "condemned to keep counting" (17:ix), which is James's extraordinary
way of saying that Marcher is obsessed with his strange, daily observance
of the future (or of what James later calls Marcher's "fortune" [17:x]).
The preface foretells the story in some detail, comparing the anticlimax
of Marcher's fate to economic failure: "His career thus resolves itself into
a great negative adventure, my report of which presents, for its centre,
the fine case that has caused him most tormentedly to 'burn' [to feel his
extraordinary fate at hand], and then most unprofitably to stray" (17:x–xi).
Like Stransom, Marcher's observance of destiny is really obsession with loss,
and loss registers in this instance in both spiritual and economic discourse.
And like Stransom, Marcher is not aware of the role that absence plays in his
obsessive fretting until the end of his drama. Throughout the lives of these
sensitive gentlemen dead loss is signified by signs that first suggest presence
(like James's diction of the marketplace). Failure to comprehend that the
beast—an image of an ominous, lurking presence—is really a figure of loss,
and failure to comprehend what it is that he loses, is the "fortune" Marcher
suffers, a fortune that James says amounts to "nothing whatever" (17:xi).

By placing "Beast in the Jungle" after "Altar of the Dead," James makes
"Beast" a reconsideration of the range of representation considered in
"Altar," one that treats his subject, particularly the underlying relationship
between the real and the irreal, anew. John Marcher, like Charles Stransom,
is a gentleman of considerable means, though perhaps not quite so well off
as Stransom. While visiting Weatherend, a country house known for its "fine
things, intrinsic features, pictures, heirlooms, treasures of all the arts . . . ;
and the great rooms [of which] were so numerous that guests could wander

at their will" (17:61), Marcher becomes reacquainted with May Bartram after several years' separation. The couple is surrounded by almost unimaginable opulence, which distracts Marcher from his companion. He cannot help observing the other visitors, who are estimating the values of Weatherend's treasures as if they were about to be sold at an estate auction. The crass actions of some, he thought, were "to be compared to the movements of a dog sniffing a cupboard" (17:62). In contrast to its effects on the curious consumers, the immense wealth surrounding Marcher filled him with a sense of history and poetry. The goods of Weatherend were art objects that spoke of a past that contributed to their intrinsic beauty and aesthetic value rather than their extrinsic value as commodities. What distinguishes Marcher from the crowd is not his ability to possess and manipulate the objects—a capability that distinguishes Stransom—but his attitude toward them. Unlike Stransom, whose superiority is derived from his extrinsic net worth, Marcher is elite because of his aesthetic sensibility.

The disparity between intrinsic and extrinsic values is shown in the opening pages of "Beast" as a difference of attitudes. These standards of value adhere to the individuals that apply them, defining, from Marcher's perspective, the value of those individuals. James is writing closer to home in the second story, for he is describing the life of a man who believes that adherence to intrinsic value (devotion to the irreal) is thoroughly superior to commodification of beauty (devotion to the real), though James, unlike Marcher, suggestively implies through his counting-house diction that the sacred can be comprehended by the discourse of the profane. Although Marcher's stance might be a natural one for an artist whose works have not brought him much financial gain, and compatible with James's temperament, through "Beast" James ultimately rejects Marcher's attitude as devotion to dead loss that is just as fruitless as Stransom's materialistic devotion to the same.

Devotion to the intrinsic leads to total self-absorption. In "Altar of the Dead," Stransom is joined at his altar by another worshiper, a woman who, he learns, "earned money by her pen, writing under a pseudonym she never disclosed in magazines he never saw" (17:29). Stransom avoided signs of her reality, preferring to think of her only as an image and supplement of his own. The narrator explains that "her visible industry was a convenience to him; it helped his contented thought of her, the thought that rested in the dignity of her proud obscure life, her little remunerated art and her little impenetrable home" (17:29). Her assumed lack of income, her dependence on what he chooses to believe is a little-appreciated art (and appreciation in Stransom's lexicon is a synonym for income), and especially the presence of "her decayed relative"—an aging aunt whose presence in the rooms shared with her niece forbids company—qualify this mourner to be "priestess of his altar" (17:29). Unlike Mary Antrim, she has little value in the discourse of economy; she is not the signpost of a man's financial prowess, and circumstances disallow intimacy with her. Her presence at the altar, in other words, will never detract from the two things it represents: dead loss and Stransom's undivided attention to it, as to an image of himself. Moreover, according to Stransom's perceptions, she has no apparent desire for wealth nor any immediate concerns about need. In fact, in her appearance Stransom discerns little except her ability to contribute: "She was n't, the mourning niece, in her first youth, and her vanished freshness had left something behind that, for Stransom, represented the proof it had been tragically sacrificed. Whatever she gave him the assurance of she gave without references. She might have been a divorced duchess—she might have been an old maid who taught the harp" (17:25). Stransom perceives her as someone who has sacrificed to another in the past, and who gives to him now (gives *assurance*, which translates into the discourse of economy as *insurance*). The absence of a perceivable past, like the assumed absence of need and desire, makes her an object of perfect blankness—like a sheet of paper—on which his own needs, desires, and memories are inscribed.

Marcher's dim memory produces a similar enabling blankness when he meets May Bartram. Marcher slips into conversation with May Bartram initially as an escape from those enjoying their commodity fetishism, but quickly finds in her a view to his own history. While her face was for Marcher "a reminder, yet not quite a remembrance," she had not lost the thread of their past (17:62). He sought from her, at first, what he found in the objects about him: a sense of the past and of its beauty, not any particular intimacy with the individual behind it. Yet Marcher is startled to learn that the past he shared with May Bartram was both remarkably intimate (he had confided in her his greatest secret) and even more remarkably forgotten (he had no memory of ever confiding in her or, for that matter, in anyone). The only detail of their first meeting that Marcher recalls is that it took place in the palace of the Caesars. Thus this tale begins with a confluence of materialism, personal history, Marcher's loss of origin (of their relationship), and intimacy that recalls the beginning pages of both "Altar," which recount the origin of Stransom's temple, and the preface. Amid the background of valuable objects and a crowd consumed by commodity fetishism, May recalls a specific historical narrative, though she apparently does not incite

Marcher's aesthetic appreciation. Yet May must do all the work. Like James, Marcher refords the stream of time only to come back emptyhanded; May, on the other hand, remembers in detail conversations from ten years earlier. Marcher's capacity for intimacy is called into question by his inability to recall May and their earlier interactions; as a result, one wonders if he too replaces human intimacy with aestheticism. In fact, Stransom's economic value system, which allows him to reduce people to controllable objects, is transformed in this story into Marcher's aesthetic value system, which allows him to reduce people, including perhaps himself, to objects whose values are based not on what they are worth extrinsically, but on how they function (how they act, what service they can provide, and so forth) within his own frame of personal reference, which is to say that for Marcher, significant people are signs within his semiotic field.[12] As signs, people have for Marcher an intrinsic value within his irreal construction of himself; therefore a person's worth depends entirely on the degree of beauty and truth that that person connotes to Marcher.

Admitting others into the circle of privileged economic ability and aesthetic consciousness disturbs both Stransom and Marcher; by acknowledging an Other, each man must at least momentarily turn his gaze from the Self. By reducing others to signs, whether in a discourse about the real or the irreal, both Stransom and Marcher attempt to keep themselves masters of their self-defined semiotic fields. Stransom's closest relationship is materialistic, for materialism precludes intimacy and enhances control. When her aging aunt dies, Stransom's priestess inherits her "tiny fortune" and freedom of the house, albeit in a slum (17:33). But her freedom to extend their communion to her home is worrisome. When his fellow worshiper expresses her desire to further their relationship, if only to spend more time together away from the altar, Stransom is "rather chilled . . . for they had been happy together as they were" (17:33). He fears that his companion's

---

12. In *Nietzsche, James, and the Artistic Will* (New York: Oxford University Press, 1978), Stephen Donadio has argued that in "The Beast in the Jungle," "the general presence of the physical world is virtually eliminated; . . . the weight of that world is felt only insofar as particular material objects may be seen as possessing symbolic value, reflecting on an external plane the essential situation of the characters." Donadio further explains, however, "that in works of this kind the physical world no longer serves as a hard, factual alternative to a fluid psychological state: on the contrary, the external world has a tendency to mirror the preoccupations of the character, and everything perceived seems to reduce itself into an inventory of the contents of his mind" (105–6). Donadio's argument supports my own in this respect, suggesting that materialism, which is essentially egotistical, replaces intimacy, which is other-directed.

freedom in the house might make a "difference . . . somehow . . . very great and would consist of still other things than her having let him come in" (17:33). Stransom's desire for what he thinks of as intimacy allows no room for reciprocity, and it is expressed in images of materialism. His desire for intimacy is desire for complete control, the sort of control that one can have over inanimate objects only: when Stransom imagines himself suspending a string of pearls on Mary Antrim's neck, he does not imagine, we should note, Mary moving, speaking, or in any other way responding. She is effectively (and affectively) dead even in his imagination's resurrection of her. Similarly, Stransom seems to appreciate his friends far more after they have died and been replaced by candles. The candles are more comfortable companions than their human signifieds ever were. The fear that his companion may somehow offer herself to him as more than the priestess of the altar sends Stransom into near panic: in her home, their relationship might be guided by her desires.

John Marcher and May Bartram develop an understanding that is first based on her knowledge of his prevision that one day he will meet a singular, dramatic fate, and that in light of this knowledge she "neither chaffed him nor betrayed him" (17:75). But the understanding does not develop into a friendship, really, until the death of May's great-aunt, who had been May's guardian and who, like the aging relative of Stransom's fellow mourner, left her niece an income that was modest yet sufficient to enable May "to set up a small home in London" (17:75). James's predilection for gentlemen so sensitive that the rigors of the everyday world chafe them, is matched, one would believe after reading both "Altar" and "Beast," by an equally strong predilection for sexlessly pairing these gentlemen with dependent nieces of aging aunts who die and in death bequeath those nieces modest incomes and leave them home alone—two very real changes that suddenly enable intimacy (intimacy that is avoided or replaced by the gentlemen's strange observances). These pairs never marry: Stransom and his companion are never emotionally intimate until, perhaps (and arguably), his death; Marcher is too sensitive and too thoughtful a gentleman, the narrator tells us, to ask May Bartram to marry and therefore to share his ominous fate—it would be like asking "a lady on a tiger-hunt" (17:79). In other words, Marcher carefully attends to his potential future rather than to his relationship with May. After all, asking May to sit by his side and watch for the beast *is* asking a lady on a tiger hunt, whether Marcher's relationship with her is sexually intimate or not. When Marcher does think of his relationship with her, Marcher thinks of himself as "the most harmless of maniacs" and of

May as "his kind wise keeper, unremunerated but fairly amused and, in the absence of other near ties, not disreputably occupied" (17:81). May's reward is amusement; Marcher, in turn, is tended to. Just as Stransom makes gifts to his companion, Marcher offers May material rewards as well as amusement in spite of his claim that May is unremunerated. The couple had known each other long enough to develop "a hundred small traditions," but the one cited by the narrator as an example is Marcher's gift to May on her birthday of a small but relatively expensive trinket. The gift does not connote heterosexual bonding (as Stransom's imagined gift of pearls does, given the tradition of the adornment of women to signify male economic prowess); it signifies to Marcher "that he had n't sunk into real selfishness" (17:84). His momentary, annual thoughtfulness allowed his self-absorption to continue unabated year after year. Yet just as Stransom's pearls signify Mary Antrim's relative value to Stransom, Marcher's gift is a tacit reminder that May Bartram is valuable enough to him to at least momentarily displace his observation of fate, yet not so singly valuable to incite him to spend emotional energy on her and give her what she truly desires and deserves. Moreover, by offering May Bartram what is in effect a salary for her efforts as his companion, John Marcher raises the value of his perpetual observation by relieving it of its appearance of narcissism and neglect of May; he identifies May's actions as those of an employee, or perhaps of a prostitute of emotion. Marcher expresses his devotion to intrinsic value in very real terms. Those who fall within the frame of his identity, as May has, quickly become objects that he, like Stransom, manipulates.

May Bartram (whose name is almost an anagram of Mary Antrim) represents, as Mary and the fellow mourner represent, the possibilities of intimacy and the realities of materialism in heterosexual relations. Stransom and Marcher become more interested personally in the mourner and May, respectively, when the women's economic futures are settled (and "settled" in both cases means improved). Yet neither gentleman takes advantage of his companion's new freedom from responsibilities to, and dependence on, her aging aunt to become more intimate. Desire may be awakened by the change of fortunes, but inability or a more forceful, conflicting emotion prevents consummation of desire. Both May and the fellow mourner appear to accept lifelong relationships that are Platonic and tied to the strange, obsessive observances that give meaning to the lives of the men. Because, however, we see them through the reflecting intelligences of the two men who are thoroughly absorbed with themselves and their relations to great absences, we never see the mourner or May very clearly (in spite of the narrators' broader moral vision). The attendant women are shown always in relation to the pressing concerns of Stransom or Marcher. Thus both women have an extrinsic value in the narrative just as the objects do that the men use to conceptualize their emotions. The mourner's value is in her role as surviving priestess of Stransom's altar: her value derives from Stransom's need for memorialization. May Bartram's value is as John Marcher's fellow observer and guardian: her value derives from Marcher's need for validation. Stransom never fully appreciate's the mourner's intrinsic value, but John Marcher does begin to appreciate the real loss that May Bartram's death has brought into his life: he reads the truth on the face of the nameless gentleman mourning in the cemetery. Marcher is able to identify what he feels and to understand the implications of those feelings by seeing them objectified on the visage of another. The revelation is channeled through a medium Marcher has from the beginning shown a penchant for understanding: Marcher reads grief and loss on the face of the gentleman mourning just as he found a remembrance in May's face, and just as he found truth and beauty in the objects at Weatherend. Marcher's translation of people into objects, which he can then read and comprehend, eventually brings him closer to the truth about himself. The beast having sprung (at this moment or at all the moments when Marcher did nothing but wait), Marcher no longer *needs* May to humanize him; he is able to comprehend her intrinsic value as he assesses the analogous loss registered in the face of another. Able to grieve for her freely, he is validated now by his own emotions.

Why then, if Stransom (and, by implication, John Marcher) commodifies the other in order to avoid intimacy, does James frame the tale by introducing Stransom as a sensitive gentleman sorely bruised by his encounters with the rough materialistic world? Before claiming that the protagonist of "Altar" is poorly suited to his society, which is "wedded by all its conditions to the immediate and the finite" (to transitory but very real objects, 17:vi), the author first considers the text itself as an object that has knocked about in the world of commodity. When art is commercially reified and derives its value exclusively from its reification, James implies, no true intimacy with art is possible (intimacy, as the tale explains it, means among other things, knowledge and appreciation). That is, when beauty is cast in terms of economic value *only*, which is derived by the relationship of supply to demand, then those who cannot unearth their literary gems (authors who cannot find editors willing to publish their works, playwrights who cannot find producers for their plays) and those who cannot afford to purchase them are restricted from the economic discourse that valorizes art. In addition, intrinsic value, which is perceived in terms of the irreal, is overlooked for created, extrinsic value—the value of what art signifies in economic discourse. In Stransom's society, aesthetic objects are commodities (the necklace, the candles, Mary's beautiful neck, for instance); their value is based on inaccessibility of ownership (demand far exceeds supply of the objects that are demanded).

James repeatedly experienced, however, that sad reality that inaccessibility did not lend value to his work. In fact, its inaccessibility to the mainstream American literary consumer, who found James's later works in particular difficult to comprehend, rendered James's works nearly unmarketable and therefore of little economic value. James as professional artist could not afford strict devotion to the irreal, the sacred realm of Art; however, he would not sacrifice his devotion to his art and replace it with utter determination to meet consumerist demand. For James, devotion to the intrinsic must produce marketable goods in the very real world, and therefore intrinsic value and the standards by which that value is adjudged, must be compatible with—and this for James means *must be the basis of*—extrinsic value. "If art is perceived strictly in aesthetic terms," Adorno writes, "then it cannot be properly perceived in aesthetic terms. The artist must feel the presence of the empirical other in the foreground of his own experience in order to be able to sublimate that experience, thus freeing himself from his confinement to content while at the same time saving the being-for-itself of art from slipping into outright indifference toward the world."[13] Yet genuine human intimacy is as unlikely in Stransom's society as creation of art for Art's sake is impossible in the world in which James lived and wrote (regardless of the aesthetic movement at the end of the nineteenth century). A writer must eat, and critical and economic appreciation of a writer's aesthetic are both sustenance. The consuming world did not immediately recognize the intrinsic value of James's manuscript just as Stransom could not appreciate the intrinsic beauty of his companion. Her neck might not have been the best showplace for a string of priceless pearls, but her heart was of a greater "value" than Stransom could ever conceive.

James may have placed "The Beast in the Jungle" second in the volume so that its reinvention of Stransom's story would bring the dramatic disjunction of man and emotion that James attributes to capitalist society to some

13. Adorno, *Aesthetic Theory*, 9.

resolution. In relation to Stransom's dubious turnabout at the end of his life and story, Marcher's ability to finally appreciate the magnitude of his loss is directly linked to his superior sensitivity to aesthetic value. Whereas for Stransom physical objects are the receptacles of his avoided emotions, for Marcher objects (of art) are replete with their own meaning. Stransom's relation to the world is essentially narcissistic: the world is his mirror. To at least some degree, Marcher is able to comprehend meaning and value that does not merely reflect his own (meaning and value). The opening scene at Weatherend aggressively establishes this difference between protagonists. This difference is registered in the preface, moreover, when James's concern with economy shifts from discussion of thematic and formal concerns to direct semantic representation.

James again reinvents aspects of the conflict between intrinsic and extrinsic, or aesthetic and commercial, value in "The Birthplace," the third and last story in this range of representation. In this tale, "another poor gentleman— of interest as being yet again too fine for his rough fate" (17:xi), engages in a conflict between economic necessity and the integrity he ascribes to historical truth. Underlying this conflict are the relation between truth and beauty, which ultimately describes the intrinsic value of art, and the relation between art's intrinsic value and its extrinsic (indeed, monetary) value in the life of the artist.[14] The preface frames this story as it does the previous two, by displacing the tale of origin with the tale's history as a failed commodity: in spite of the perfect mating of theme and form (the *nouvelle*, as James calls it), "The Birthplace" was begun by James with a "certainty that

14. The traditional interpretation of this story is well represented by Jan W. Dietrichson in *The Image of Money in the American Novel of the Gilded Age* (New York: Humanities Press, 1969): "The power of money in the life of the little man is clearly demonstrated in this ironical story, not least its power to make him disregard the dictates of his moral conscience. A person without independent wealth is not a free moral agent" (148). Dietrichson's reading of "The Birthplace" interprets Morris Gedge as a "little man" who "deliberately distorts and falsifies truth . . . to please his masters." Thus he views the story as a damnation of capitalist society and assumes that naked fact is intrinsically more valuable than any aesthetic transformation of fact into fiction or dramatic performance. When a man must "disregard the dictates of his moral conscience" in order to survive, Dietrichson explains, then he "is not a free moral agent" (148): the system has utterly subsumed the individual. While such a reading might be plausible if "The Birthplace" is considered in isolation, the preface and the accumulating presence of the conceptual framework of the volume denies that Gedge's reconception of his performance is either immoral or disempowering. In fact, the "damning" performance that Gedge effects toward the end of the tale is what makes him most authorial. The wonderment of his strange American friends and the monetary remuneration he finally receives attests to his ability to succeed aesthetically and commercially.

it would nowhere, at the best (a prevision not falsified) find 'acceptance' "
(17:xii). The tale, in other words, was without extrinsic value even though
it was unequivocally a formal success. The irony is as purposeful as it is
marked. While in his previous discussions of "Altar" and "Beast" James noted
the harshness of material reality, particularly as it affected the production
of art, he nevertheless noted the eventual attribution of material value to
those tales, suggesting that in time extrinsic value grew to reflect intrinsic
value. "The Birthplace" is, according to the preface, perfect in its way, yet
of the least demonstrable material value of the first three tales. In this case,
there is absolutely no correlation between intrinsic and extrinsic values, and
James foresaw this disparity, he says, before he even began writing the tale.
James certainly recognized the difference between what sells and what does
not, and in the face of such knowledge he chose to write "The Birthplace,"
electing to create something of high intrinsic value but no extrinsic value
whatsoever rather than to sacrifice a degree of the former to gain a degree
of the latter.

The profound disparity between intrinsic and extrinsic values that James
describes in the preface raises the question of whether one reflects *true* value
and the other does not (which is to ask whether value is relative or absolute).
The answer, as Adorno would predict, is not in what might seem for an artist
the obvious selection of intrinsic, aesthetic grounds as the proper location
of true value. It is found in a complete reconsideration of the very terms of
inquiry. In this story, James says,

> in the highest degree were the conditions reproduced for that mystic,
> that "chemical" change wrought in the impression of life by its ded-
> ication to an aesthetic use. . . . Beautiful on all this ground exactly,
> to the projector's mind, the process by which the small cluster of
> actualities latent in the fact reported to him was to be reconstituted
> and, so far as they might need, altered; the felt fermentation, ever
> interesting, but flagrantly so in the example before us, that enables
> the sense originally communicated to make fresh and possibly quite
> different terms for the new employment there awaiting it. (17:xii)

The apparently dialectical conflict between intrinsic and extrinsic value gives
way in James's rhetoric to, if not a conflict, at least a sometimes tumultuous
transformation of the world and all its signifying facts into Art, where truth
and true value no longer have meaning as they do in the extraliterary world,

but rather mean only as they are reconstructed by the "projector" to the "actualities" that truth and value signify.[15]

As James takes up his discussion of "The Birthplace," the running commentary on intrinsic and extrinsic value is suddenly focused on the artist himself, the person who transforms fact into art. The "'chemical' change wrought in the impression of life by its dedication to an aesthetic use," shifts the reader's focus to the transformative powers of art on the life of the artist and in turn, on the artist's transformed and transforming impression of life. The subject of the passage is the *process* of transformation, not the transformation itself. "The Birthplace" offers an example of "felt fermentation," James says. The change in Morris Gedge, like his reconstitution of the meager facts of the great poet's life into a dramatic monologue, is a change of perspective on his own life to one that encompasses appreciation for both the intrinsic and extrinsic values of art. This broadened perspective ultimately liberates Gedge from his indenture to the intrinsic—the unknowable past—and introduces him to the real and the palpable present. "The Birthplace" makes the relation of art to history a moral issue, and it validates subjective truth (the aesthetic transformation of fact) in the face of objective truth (the practical portrayal of fact) in the consciousness of the individual dedicated to the aesthetic life. Moreover, it gives great real value to this transformation of the real into the irreal—the transformation of fact into elaborate fiction.

When Morris and Isabel Gedge first begin their duties as caretakers of a great poet's birthplace, they are entirely dependent on their salary. The birthplace is a business and a treasured site that is funded primarily by tourists who pay admission and expect to be guided through the rooms where the nameless poet was born and raised. The financial success of the poet's home as a tourist attraction depends largely on the Gedges' performance—their recitation of history conceived from legends of the poet's early life. Yet when the new caretakers first arrive at the birthplace, Morris Gedge's expectations for the position are greatly exaggerated. Similar to the scenes at the beginning of "Altar" and "Beast," the beginning of "The Birthplace" establishes the elitism of its central male character.

---

15. Adorno recognizes a similar transformation, which he characterizes as a dismantling of the opposition between the sacred and the profane: "The profane secularizes the sacred realm to the point where the latter is the only secular thing left. The sacred realm is thus objectified, staked out as it were, because its moment of untruth awaits secularization as much as it tries to avert it through incantation" (*Aesthetic Theory,* 8).

The couple had been selected from among the throngs of "applicants, candidates, besiegers of the door of every one supposed to have a voice in the matter"; a sense of almost divine selection motivated Morris Gedge to prepare for what he thought would be an intimacy with the great poet that would transform himself and his world: "The shining spaces surrounded [Gedge]; the association alone gave a nobler arch to the sky" (17:131–32, 136). Isabel Gedge's response is of a different caliber. She understands the fundamental economic relationship into which they were entering: "She looked at [her husband's] face, and her own lighted as if he had suddenly grown handsome. 'Certainly—we shall live as in a fairy-tale. But what I mean is that we shall give, in a way—and so gladly—quite as much as we get. With all the rest of it we're for instance neat' " (17:136–37). In his delusion, Morris Gedge rises to a great calling as he devotes his life to aesthetic use. Realistically, Isabel Gedge sees the potential remuneration for a job well done. He focuses on the unnamed and ultimately unknowable poet—a transcendental irreality; she focuses on her husband first, and then on the contingency of a trade relationship with their very real employer.

Devotions to the real and irreal are engendered in "The Birthplace" to a far greater extent than they are in either "Altar" or "Beast." James shows that one devoted to either extreme, even if wed to his or her antithesis, is doomed to suffer the profound limitations of vision that characterize Stransom and Marcher. The engendering extends to distinction of the physical locations of the Gedges' devotions. Once they become situated as caretakers of the birthplace, Mr. Gedge's need to feel intimate with the "Presence" of the great poet drives him to prowl the birthplace at night, after the doors are locked to visitors, and Mrs. Gedge has retired to their nearby cottage. These strange pilgrimages bring Gedge, "or ought to have brought him, he seemed to see, nearer to the enshrined Presence, enlarging the opportunity for communion and intensifying the sense of it. His wife, in contrast, rejoiced in the distinctness, contiguous though it was, of their own little residence, where she trimmed the lamp and stirred the fire and heard the kettle sing, repairing the while the omissions of the small domestic who slept out; she foresaw herself, with some promptness, drawing rather sharply the line between her own precinct and that in which the great spirit might walk. . . . And she vaguely imaged the development of a domestic antidote after a while, precisely, in the shape of curtains more markedly drawn and everything most modern and lively, tea, 'patterns,' the newspapers, the female fiction" that she had been unable to read at their previous position because it was frowned upon by her employers

(17:151–52). Both visions of life at the birthplace attempt to exclude and thereby devalue the other. Mr. Gedge seeks initiation into a pantheon of aesthetic greatness, while Mrs. Gedge hopes and works for independence and freedom within the confines of her own happy sublunary home. Morris Gedge favors the quiet, dark irreality of the ghostly poet's sanctuary, whereas Isabel Gedge enjoys continuous commerce with the very real objects of her lighted, heated dwelling.

Yet from the first intimation that the position would be offered them, Morris Gedge builds his intimacy with the eternally unseen Presence on what he perceives to be very real facts: he and Mrs. Gedge read everything they can find on the man. As the previous caretaker, Miss Putchin, points out, fact gives Gedge authority over the paying visitors by arming him with truth, to which all conflicting perspectives must yield: " 'there are the facts. Otherwise where would any of us be? That's all you've got to go upon. A person, however cheeky, can't have them *his* way just because he takes it into his head. There can be only *one* way, and,' she gaily added as she took leave of them, 'I'm sure it's quite enough!' " (17:148–49). Facts are signifiers in the real world, but Gedge acts as if knowledge of the facts of the Poet's life invests him with rights to a particular intimacy with the Presence and control over the present. In this way he mimics James's use of the tales of origin as instigators of his authority over the reading of the text:

> The Holy of Holies of the Birthplace was the low, the sublime Chamber of Birth. . . . It was as empty as a shell of which the kernel has withered, and contained neither busts nor prints nor early copies; it contained only the Fact—*the* Fact itself—which, as he stood sentient there at midnight, our friend, holding his breath, allowed to sink into him. He *had* to take it as the place where the spirit would most walk and where He would therefore be most to be met, with possibilities of recognition and reciprocity. (17:153–54)

Facts are the only signs of the Poet, really of Gedge's relationship to the Poet. Without them, just as his predecessor implied, he would be nowhere (of any emotional, social, commercial, personal, or literary value). But the facts are intangible signs of an *absent* signified; they decorate the frame of absence and denote absence as what is in this tale repeatedly called "Presence"— without the frame of facts, the Presence might not exist in the real world. Devotion to the irreal Other brings Gedge self-esteem; therefore, possession of the frame is for him possession of the only available sign of authority.

When Mr. and Mrs. Hayes, young, wealthy American tourists, visit the birthplace just before closing—just before Gedge begins his midnight haunt —and question the existence of verifiable facts of the poet's life, the frame of Gedge's authority crumbles, and Gedge's self-esteem plummets. If Gedge cannot commune with the unknowable past, he cannot perceive value in his present existence. The Hayeses are able to shake the foundation of Gedge's authority for several reasons. They recognize Gedge's dual roles as historian and dramatist; they arrive at the very hour when Gedge is transformed from showman to seeker of Truth; and they acknowledge Gedge's authority before they question its source. Gedge had always been intimidated, or at least more easily influenced, by those who appeared to know more than he did. That is why the previous caretaker's last words go to his heart. These strange American tourists seem to possess the ultimate truth—that there is no absolute truth at all, only the invention of truth.

Very much like the Aspern scholar, who is divided between his roles as historian of fact and author of invention, Gedge becomes split between devotion to a signified that has lost its signifier, and loathing of his own invention: he finds himself "splitting into halves, unmistakeably—he who, whatever else he had been, had at least always been so entire and in his way so solid. One of the halves, or perhaps even, since the split promised to be rather unequal, one of the quarters, was the keeper, the showman, the priest of the idol; the other piece was the poor unsuccessful honest man he had always been" (17:161–62). His finds himself in a double bind. He does not value his own transformation of the irreal into the real (his dramatic performance at the birthplace). The facts of the poet vindicate his roles as keeper and showman, while the facts of his existence—poverty, failure, and honesty—disempower him regardless of his position as priest of the idol. From the very beginning, Morris Gedge is using his devotion to one set of facts about an Other to overcome a set of facts about the Self. His search for Truth, then, is tainted at the start by its necessitating and prerequisite denial of truth. And when the facts of the poet prove false, the facts of Gedge's existence pronounce themselves all too forcefully.

Mrs. Gedge, on the other hand, seeks her happiness in the ability to manipulate and control the physical objects about her: reading a book that had once been forbidden to her, drawing curtains closed—being the mistress of her house, domestic life, and free time. But her happiness is contingent on the position she shares with her husband. If he fails in his duties, they both will suffer the consequences. Her preference for the physical world, for concrete reality, is never offered by James as a preferable, more honest approach to life than Gedge's search for value exclusively in the realm of irreality. In fact, her existence is so thoroughly entrenched in physical reality that she has little or no aesthetic sense, no ability to invent; most important, she has no real power. Mrs. Gedge is completely dependent on her "superiors," and these seem to include everyone in the story. Her husband is empowered to lose her security (and eventually to double their income); her employer may discharge her or not, at his leisure and whim; and her previous employer maintained the power to censor her reading material. Even the Hayeses have power over Mrs. Gedge; they can influence her husband whereas she cannot. Mrs. Gedge is helpless except in her own home, and this is on loan from her employer and therefore contingent on her husband's willingness to perform.

Gedge eventually learns what James has declared in preface after preface. Facts are commodities to be used and then discarded by the person like Gedge devoted to the aesthetic life. As James says in the preface to *The Aspern Papers*, the historian wants more facts than he can possibly discover while the novelist wants fewer facts than he has. The kind and quantity of facts has nothing to do with Gedge's personal or moral value, according to James. What he does with those facts—what he makes of them or of the absence of them—will determine who and what he is. Gedge's choices, in this light, are clear: he can be a historian silenced by the absence of validating facts, or he can become an artist, and find glory in the absence. In response to his sudden indeterminacy caused by the indeterminacy of absolute truth, Gedge creates a performance so singularly compelling, so completely of his own invention, that Mrs. Gedge fears her husband is mad and worse, that her employer will hear of his outlandish behavior and fire them. Gedge himself does not seem to appreciate the empowering decision he has made. The American visitors return to see the results of their first visit, and they are impressed by Gedge's dramatic monologue though they too are concerned that Gedge's employer will be dissatisfied with the performance that seems to displace the poet himself as the attraction of the birthplace. Only Morris Gedge, whose devotion to the intrinsic persists, fails to appreciate what more he stands to lose.

In the preface, James substitutes histories of the tales as commodities for the facts of their origins and development. That is, facts of the tales are replaced by discussion of remuneration for aesthetic performance. It should not be surprising, then, in light of the persistent previsions of the preface, that Gedge's dramatic performance is materially rewarded by his employer. After all, the show's profits were increased. Furthermore, Gedge's

performance, as we see through the eyes of his special American visitors, has
intrinsic, aesthetic value. Like "The Birthplace," Gedge's performance is the
perfect fusion of content and form—the necessary fusion, Adorno argues,
if Art is to be valorized in the profane world. Gedge succeeds, it seems, at
what James has himself failed at: creating an artwork (a dramatic one, at
that) that has both intrinsic and extrinsic value. Nothing at the end of the
tale equivocates Morris Gedge's success. Isabel Gedge becomes inarticulate
with joy when she learns that their stipend has been doubled. The leisured
Hayeses unite with their laboring counterparts: Mrs. Hayes jumps to kiss
Mrs. Gedge; Mr. Hayes silently shakes Mrs. Gedge's hand. Significantly, the
"very echoes of the Birthplace were themselves, for the instant, hushed," and
Gedge has the last word: "'And there *you* are!" (17:213). Gedge, perhaps,
finally meets the Poet, at least in his own performance of the Poet's life,
because he attributes intrinsic value to his ability to invent such an artful
drama and to be equally successful in the marketplace. And as a poet, he
not only makes the irreal register in the real (by reconstructing the Poet and
getting paid for it), but he transforms the real into Art. When he returns
from his meeting with his employer, Grant-Jackson, Morris Gedge sees his
wife sitting between Mr. and Mrs. Hayes. "The three together had at any
rate the effect of recalling to him—it was too whimsical—some picture, a
sentimental print, seen and admired in his youth, a 'Waiting for the Verdict,'
a 'Counting the Hours,' or something of that sort; humble respectability in
suspense about humble innocence" (211).

Perfect coincidence of intrinsic and extrinsic value in relations with others
and in conceptions of the self is the goal of the conceptual frame of this
first section of the volume. The perfect coincidence ultimately places the
work of the artist over either the world it transforms or the art that is its
transformation. "The Birthplace" contributes to the conceptual frame its
responses to the questions of value that frame the tale. In the realm of the
real, intrinsic value is subjective and self-referential: Gedge's self-esteem,
though based on knowledge of facts, is ultimately determined by Gedge
himself. Extrinsic value is determined by the marketplace: what Gedge's
performance earns is determined solely by Gedge's employer. In the realm
of the intrinsic, value reflects an ideal. It has both intrinsic and extrinsic
standards of measurement that do not always coincide because the intrinsic
can be known only as it is registered on the real, and the real introduces
the possibility of imperfect correlation. If Gedge's performance had been
unpopular with his employer, its aesthetic value would have been just as
great though unremunerated. Thus truth and value are relative insofar as

they are either intrinsic or extrinsic. Whether either has an independent third determination that is absolute is a question neither James nor "The Birthplace" will answer.

Yet through the agency of the preface James does suggest an answer to the most pressing question: How should James's reader understand the stories in this volume? While the often conflicting relations of intrinsic and extrinsic values are evident in each of the first three stories, James's intention that the reader see each of the stories as part of a process of thought about value is not so clear. The preface encourages a reading that constantly recalls the author as the source of wondering, and the author's wondering as the origin of the tale. The author's experience as a merchant of art also becomes an important frame of reference by which the reader will interpret the stories. The semiotic field of the first "range of representation," framed by the preface and expanded to include the three stories, facilitates meaning that certainly would be otherwise lost. When the meaning is retained, James has succeeded in creating his ideal reader, one who will appreciate the value of his art and show that appreciation tangibly.

James is nowhere so clearly a modernist as he is in this preface. In his assumption that language and meaning are no more perfectly related than aesthetic and economic values, he is courting if not actually creating the modern reader. Moreover, his desire for a perfect world, one in which meaning and representation are perfectly matched and in which intrinsic and extrinsic values are equivalent, is the desire of T. S. Eliot and other moderns who sought order in the fact of acknowledged chaos. What James offers to the modern reader is neither an affirmation of one system of value predicated upon a condemnation of one system of value, nor an open-handed gesture of cluelessness. He posits his own work, his own performance as the bridge between meaning and representation, between intrinsic and extrinsic, between art and the world. The next range of representation, the ghost stories that James chose to include in the Edition, takes the reader beyond the apparent conflict of values to the philosophical implications of James's focus on authorial performance.

In the Second Range of Representation: Ghostlier Demarcations and Keener Sounds

The ghost tales that make up the second range of represention in volume 17 take the objects of the author's wondering one step beyond the resolution that "The Birthplace" seems to offer. If identities are doubled—that is, if people and art have both intrinsic and extrinsic values—and if, conse-quently, truth is relative and therefore not only never absolute but often multiplied, how can the frame of consciousness be expanded to account for and to include this exponentially expanding conception of existence? In the second range of representation, corporeal reality, so well championed by Isabel Gedge, is intermingled with the uncorporeal (or with an alternate reality) as a way of creating juxtaposed images of reality and irreality that co-exist in the same plane. Presence and absence are coupled both as signs of one another and as contingent aspects of individual consciousness. In the first three stories in volume 17, the individuals trapped in the real world are continually in pursuit of the irreal. In the second range of representation, James presents several successive meetings of the two worlds to imply that representation itself is the conjunction of the real and the irreal, that one world is figured in the other by its signified—the way it makes itself felt, "by recognising as their main interest some impression strongly made by them and intensely received" (17:xix). For James, irreality is most interesting when its effects in the real world are examined. When the irreal is consid-ered directly (that is, when it "constitutes the only thickness we do get") it "come[s] with an effect imperilled," for the irreal has no "intrinsic value," James says, in the real world (17:xix). As we have seen through Adorno, the aesthetic cannot be seen in aesthetic terms only. On the other hand, when irrealities are considered in the context of the real, "they most interest [us], for what we are then mainly concerned with is their imputed and borrowed dignity"—their signification in the real world.

James's rhetoric clearly relates the supernatural and art; both depend upon representation in the real world of something that is only hinted at but never seen directly. A ghost, such as that of Sir Edmund Orme, represents someone and something that are missing (in this case, the missing are an old lover and a woman's devotion to him). Its presence is a persistent reminder of those absences. James's aesthetic of fiction works in a similar way, and so his interest in the ghost story reflects his own aesthetic concerns. The world depicted in his fiction is never seen or experienced directly by the reader. It is represented as an impression on the consciousness of the central subject. James confesses to another predilection in this regard, one for "the safest arena for the play of moving accidents and mighty mutations and strange encounters, or whatever odd matters," and this is "the field . . . rather of their second than of their first exhibition" (17:xix). To grasp anything directly is to leave the irreal realm of art and enter the realm of reality; therefore, James's fiction will always remain within the field of secondhand phenomena, by which, he says, "I mean nothing more cryptic than I feel myself show them best by showing almost exclusively the way they are felt, by recognising as their main interest some impression strongly made by them and intensely received" (17:xix). The world in the fiction is imputed by the subject consciousness at the center of the narrative. What the reader receives, therefore, is a ghost of what the subject consciousness presumably has experienced. The narrative offers up a ghostly image of what exists in another realm altogether, and which the reader can never contact. The lesson in the preface is a lesson on Jamesian aesthetics. It encourages the reader to consider the ghost tales in the second range of representation as horrific fairy tales, and as allegories about the nature of James's literary representation. Perhaps nowhere else in the Edition does James transform his fiction into self-conscious works of art that reflect the work of the artist, suggesting a reading of the tales that would leave plot in far distant shadows of both his artistry and his demonstration of right reading.

James implies in his prefatory discussion of the six tales of the supernatural in volume 17 that the real world becomes a text in which signs of the irreal are imprinted. However, as "The Private Life" suggests, when the real is fixed upon, we see the "text" only as the work—we see the tangible world. When the irreal is fixed upon, we see the meaning of the text: we decode the signification and lose sight of its impression. James implies that the two realms are mutually exclusive yet are utterly contingent. In fact, "The Private Life," the first of the ghost stories, involves, James says, "two distinct and alternate presences, the assertion of either of which on any occasion directly involved the entire extinction of the other" (17:xiii). When Clare Vawdrey, "the greatest (in the opinion of many) of our literary glories," is confronted socially, he is "the fresh sane man, illustrious and undistinguished—no 'sensitive poor gentleman' he!," but he is decidedly not the great genius who has "written the immortal things" that made his literary reputation (17:xiii). The writer-at-work and the writer-in-society are Vawdrey's alter egos that do not co-exist in one body, but exist separately, simultaneously, and dialectically. The writer-at-work lives in solitude, unseen, creating art. The writer-in-society is always and only seen; he gives voice to the other's text (the real signifying the irreal). In the real world of the writer-in-society, the writer-at-work is irreal, for he exists only in the signs of his work—his texts—and is always otherwise absent. Yet he is always being referred to by the work he produces and its presentation by his alter ego.

The writer-at-work remains invisible, producing art of great value; according to the preface, however, value exists only in the relation of the irreal to the real—the relation of the writer-at-work to the writer-in-society, whose value is entirely extrinsic. That relation is made by the texts themselves, whose origins and signifieds are embodiments of the author. James confounds this team, and the relationship between the real and the irreal that it symbolizes, by making the invisible writer visible to the snooping actress Blanche Adney, who creeps up on the writer-at-work while others (off the page) keep the writer-in-society busy entertaining. Yet while Mrs. Adney would prefer the survival of the struggling artist over the social presence who commodifies the other's work, the co-conspiring narrator provides the voice of authorial truth, explaining that both embodiments are "'members of a firm, and one of them would never be able to carry on the business without the other. Moreover mere survival would be dreadful for either'" (17:250). Mrs. Adney would choose one realm and banish the other forever to a disconnected, unregistering nonexistence. She would therefore rob the irreal of its existence as it is signified by the real and make it immediate and, as James says, imperiled. There would be no writer-in-society to commodify (and vivify) the works of his other; as a result Mrs. Adney would find herself the recipient of art that has intrinsic but no extrinsic value, no ability to be commodified (and, therefore, no chance that she will be cast in Vawdrey's next successful drama). The narrator explains why: the writer-at-work "'has no passions'" (17:251), no commerce with the physical, sensual, real world. He creates signs that replace him in that world, just as Mrs. Adney, when she is performing on stage, becomes characters that replace her. (It is for this reason that she feels so drawn to the writer-at-work.) The writer-in-society, however, is all passions, all senses, all very real and very present. He has no commerce with irreality except when he reads aloud from the work of his double. He is thoroughly engaged in the real world: he hears the applause at the end of his plays and he collects the royalty checks.

The allegorical reading established by the preface lies close to the surface of the story. Just as the elimination of one member of the firm would result in an end of its business, elimination of either represented meaning or its representation would result in an end of art. Literature can not, James asserts, do away with its role as aesthetic mediation between two realms. It can not present directly, it can only re-present. To do otherwise is to shatter irreality and to leave reality aesthetically bankrupt. Moreover, the irreal requires the real, for the irreal "has no passions": it does not create meaning; it represents it.

In "The Private Life" James seems to return to a stance from which he can view the relation between reality and irreality as bipolar, though certainly contingent and not oppositional. The relation is enacted in this story, however, through the agency of the work of art, which may explain why James placed "The Private Life" first in the series of ghost stories even though it is the least ghostly. Even without the preface to encourage an allegorical reading, the tale gestures in that direction. The allegorical register is most accessible here. The real and the irreal are not in conflict. Instead, they are imaged in this story as two distinct bodies that assume the same identity, suggesting that the relation between art and the world constitutes the whole of which both art and world are parts. Self and other, moreover, are paradoxically both dialectical and the same. The writer-in-society and the writer-at-work are never together, yet together they constitute Clare Vawdrey.

"Owen Wingrave," "The Friends of the Friends," "Sir Edmund Orme," "The Real Right Thing," and "The Jolly Corner" follow "The Private Life," and complete the second range of representation. Each story presents a confrontation of the real and the irreal, and in each story the irreal—figured as the supernatural—is some irrecoverable, unchangable past or some alternate self that is true and yet that exists only as it is signified in the alternately true reality. In "Owen Wingrave" irreality is exhibited only by its most dramatic effect, the death of Owen Wingrave after his confrontation behind closed doors with the reality of legend, whereas in "The Friends of the Friends," irreality is presented as the suspicions of a jealous woman that her fiancé and the spirit of her deceased friend rendezvous each evening. The fairy tales, as James calls these stories, offer a range of representation that explores other dimensions of the reality-irreality, extrinsic-intrinsic, presence-absence, self-other dualities that are made approximations of one another and of the relation of art and the world.

"Owen Wingrave" offers several glimpses of the irreal as the realm in which lost or absent elements of the reality are stored. Owen Wingrave, who refuses to follow family tradition and enter the military, has an older brother who is "literally imbecile and banished from view; deformed, unsocial, irretrievable, he had been relegated to a private asylum and had become among the friends of the family only a little hushed lugubrious legend" (17:279). Institutionalization of the eldest son makes Owen, in effect, the sole heir to the family fortune and, more important, heir to the heap of family expectations that otherwise might have been doled out in very unequal portions between the two boys, Owen receiving the meager share. Extrinsic value is in this story made a curse: the great wealth that Owen will inherit by default of primogeniture is the tangible sign of the required suppression of all that he is and believes. Possession of the family fortune means extinction of Owen and in his place, the creation of the Wingrave Heir. The brothers, one absent and one present, are distinctly doubled: Owen's decision against the military threatens to disgrace the family, who would in response banish him, making Owen as irreal as his elder brother—irreal except as a family legend.

As it is in "The Birthplace," legend in this tale is the single most effective way of contacting irreality because it is the reflection in reality of the irreal, just as the writer-at-work's texts, particularly as they are read aloud by the writer-in-society, signify the writer-at-work in the world. Legend—one product of the transformation of fact—becomes the receptacle for all that is lost and discarded; legend is also the treasurehouse of family values and beliefs. Legends of his ancestors' military heroism have haunted Owen since his childhood. He chooses against those legends, denying the values that have elevated his predecessors' actions to such high estate in family memory.

Legend also provides a pre-text for Owen's story. Early in the second chapter, Mr. Coyle, Owen's instructor, recounts the romance of Owen's aunt Miss Wingrave and Captain Hume-Walker, the brother of Miss Wingrave's closest friend, Mrs. Julian. Miss Wingrave's jealous, demanding nature forced her friend's brother to return to active military service and eventually meet his death in the Indian Mutiny. As both a reminder and a consolation, Miss Wingrave asked Mrs. Julian and her young daughter to remain with her at Paramore, the family estate. This legend implicates both the military life and the Julians in the story of Owen Wingrave's death that follows: Owen spends his last fateful night in a room normally locked at sunset—a room at night normally accessible, that is, like the past, only by legend and history. The room is supposedly haunted by the Wingrave ancestory, and Owen shuts himself in after the others have gone to bed to prove his bravery to Mrs. Julian's daughter, now a young and very beautiful woman. The next morning Owen is found dead, "all the young soldier on the gained field" (17:319). Facing the irreality encoded in legend, as Owen does, is facing the truth of his existence: that it is immediately contingent on his brother's exile and more generally on his ancestors' successes on the battlefield. Owen chooses not to value the role vacated in his brother's absence and the military life that created it, thus rejecting what is signified by the very real value of the inheritance. Yet as James's military description of Owen's corpse suggests,

Owen no longer has control of his signification: he has become another Wingrave hero, lost and then recovered through family legend.

The interpolation of Miss Wingrave's fateful spurning of Captain Hume-Walker brings the irreal into close and meaningful relation to the real; it constructs a relation between the past and the present (without imputing value to any specific knowledge of the past) that explains the present by probing the past. If Miss Wingrave had not been so jealous, Captain Hume-Walker would have remained at Paramour, might be alive, and the hopes of the Wingraves would not rest solely on Owen's shoulders. Moreover, Mrs. Julian and her daughter would probably not be living at Paramour and Owen would therefore have had no cause to prove his bravery. This version of the Wingrave history invests all the blame, and consequently all of the power, in Miss Wingrave and her cantankerous disposition. Yet Miss Wingrave did not send Owen into the haunted room; she did not cause Miss Julian to flirt with her nephew; and she did not enlist Captain Hume-Walker in the military. Owen's fate to die on the battlefield, whether the battle was fought in India or at home, was secured when Owen was born into an ancestral line of military men who died military deaths and became representations through familial (predominantly female-repeated) legends. The one male who did not become military was utterly silenced by imbecility and even he was transformed into legend, albeit of another kind.

Not only does history repeat itself, "Owen Wingrave" reminds its readers, but the irreal is always present and active in the real, always making itself felt as a signified. Reality frames the irreal, providing a semiotic field for its expression. The siphoning of family hopes from the eldest son to Owen must repeatedly remind the Wingraves that Owen's presence as heir signifies his brother's tragic absence. The Julians' residence at Paramour is a constant reminder of Captain Hume-Walker's death. Owen's fateful confrontation of the intrinsic responds to both signs of absence, and ultimately translates Owen himself into such an absence, inevitably another family legend. Thus it is not what actually happened in the pretextual narrative, but what the results of Miss Wingrave's action signify in the ongoing narrative (tradition) of Owen's family, that causes Owen's death.

Clearly James is presenting an ongoing struggle to find some immediate relation of real and irreal that does not depend on an intermediary such as legend. For James, the source is far less important than the representation of it. His frequent distinctions between history and literature make this point at every turn. Yet like the people referred to in the legends, the sources—those seeds of narrative—are always lurking in the shadows just beneath the narrative where James's reading discovers them sometimes all too visible. The relation between the real and the irreal, one might conclude, is not always controlled or controllable. Moreover, as "Owen Wingrave" demonstrates, neither the real nor the irreal can be avoided. The story that follows "Owen Wingrave" is "The Friends of the Friends," which relates another example of the irreal haunting the real. In this case, both real and irreal connect (perhaps even copulate), but James remains unable to picture it. The story is as simple as it is bizarre. After years of unsuccessfully trying to bring her best friend and her betrothed together to meet and become friends, the narrator finds herself in a very peculiar predicament. Her friend has died, but the narrator fears that her friend's spirit visits her fiancé's rooms every evening. It seems that union of the narrator's two friends is effected only after death has made this union in the corporeal, real world impossible. Practically speaking, the union occurs only in the narrator's imagination, for the story is told in the first person and in retrospect; the narrator recounts scenes between the man she loves and the deceased of which she cannot possibly have knowledge. These scenes are reconstructed from the signs of the irreal that have made an impression in reality; the diarist is interpreting those signs and translating them into her own dramatizations. She gives value to these signs, which is to say, she gives them power over her. The narrator confronts her fiancé with the circumstantial evidence: " 'I've watched you in silence, playing my part too; I've noted every drop in your voice, every absence in your eyes, every effort in your indifferent hand: I've waited till I was utterly sure and miserably unhappy. How *can* you hide it when you're abjectly in love with her, when you're sick almost to death with the joy of what she gives you' " (17:362–63). The narrator takes her own words as previsionary; as an epilogue she writes:

> He never married, any more than I've done. When six years later, in solitude and silence, I heard of his death I hailed it as a direct contribution to my theory. It was sudden, it was never properly accounted for, it was surrounded by circumstances in which—for oh I took them to pieces!—I distinctly read an intention, the mark of his own hidden hand. It was the result of a long necessity, of an unquenchable desire. To say exactly what I mean, it was a response to an irresistible call. (17:364)

From the beginning of the tale, the narrator *as author* is the conduit between reality and irreality. She indirectly unites her friends by speaking to each

of the other. She establishes the vicarious relationship in life—in reality—
that becomes direct when it becomes a union of the real (the fiancé) and
the irreal (the deceased friend). Furthermore, the narrator compulsively
interprets signs, giving them meaning and combining those meanings into
narrative. She determines that her two friends are compatible. She reads
the signs (of absence) in her lover's behavior that the two are conducting
a supernatural affair. She composes the signs surrounding her fiancé's
death into the story of his suicide. In every case, she reaches beyond the
real—beyond the signs—to the signifieds (or what she presumes are the
signifieds). All of this she does in print, transforming the irreal state of
conscious wondering into the very real state of textuality. Even the prologue
constructs a relation between the real and the irreal. James begins this tale
with a two-page, unsigned, unaddressed note, that deals with the possibilities
of publishing the tale. This prologue thereby converts the narrator's confes-
sions into a commodity, making very real what were initially only impressions
of the irreal, and thereby reminding us of the terms with which the volume
began. Ironically, the coupling of the real and the irreal, which would be
an idealized art, one in which representation and that which is represented
correspond perfectly, is never effected on the page. In fact, it is utterly
feared by the narrator who becomes obsessed with its possibilities. The
man's demise may suggest that James himself found the notion frightening.
A perfect correspondence of signs and signifieds, and therefore of art and
the world it represents, would ultimately collapse the distinction between
reality and irreality and so render the role of the artist obsolete.

In the preface James attributes the existence of these tales of the supernatural to his own love of " 'a story as a story' " that is itself a haunting: love
for each one of these tales had "from far back beset and beguiled their
author" (17:xvi). Like the Wingrave family tradition that brought Owen
to his death and the irresistable desire of the narrator of "The Friends
of the Friends" to bring her friends together just as she brings signifiers
and signifieds together, with haunting persistence these tales demanded
they be brought from the irreality of the imagination onto the page. The
appearance of the irreal in the next tale reflects James's desire to exorcise
these ghosts and gain control over them—to let them stand fully in reality
as representations so that he can take account of them and all that they
signify. Only by flushing them out and chasing them to the end, James
implies, can one be free of their nagging reminders that they also represent
absence. "Sir Edmund Orme" speaks directly to this point; this is the first
of the ghost stories in which James actually presents a ghost fully framed

by the real world. The ghost of Sir Edmund Orme appears to Mrs. Marden whenever Captain "Teddy" Bostwick courts Mrs. Marden's daughter. The ghost is a reminder to the mother that she once victimized a man in love with her and therefore was the moral cause of his suicide; it is the image of a fear that the past will repeat itself through her daughter. Sir Edmund Orme is a visitation of suppressed truth (in this case, buried truth) about Mrs. Marden that desires to be realized (to be brought into reality). As long as the possibility exists that Miss Marden might, like her mother, be nothing more than a coquette, Sir Edmund Orme will hover in the periphery. That Captain Bostwick also experiences this haunting presence is much to the ghost's credit; Sir Edmund Orme comes as a warning as well as a punishment. Charlotte Marden, in contrast, has no idea that she is strangely paired with the ghost of her mother's past; to save her from the horror of it, Captain Bostwick resolves with Mrs. Marden to prevent the presence of Sir Edmund Orme from being registered by their reactions. They refuse to signify the ghost's presence except to one another, as if the ghost (or the past) might reveal some horribly transforming truth to Charlotte Marden. Thus the two limit and control the frame in which the irreal can operate and signify in the real.

But the irreal cannot be erased. When Charlotte Marden agrees to marry Captain Bostwick, Sir Edmund Orme hovers over Mrs. Marden for a moment then disappears. As the engaged couple turns, the two discover that Mrs. Marden has died. The death of Mrs. Marden and the final exit of Sir Edmund Orme suggest that the power of the irreal cannot be contained or controlled any more than the real can be denied. Signifiers can be manipulated and framed, but meaning, like value, transgresses all enclosures: it is imputed and borrowed; it is not inherent. In fact, the attempts of Mrs. Marden and Captain Bostwick to contain the irreal actually allow the irreal to make its indelible mark. Mrs. Marden might not have encouraged her daughter to marry had she not had the specter of her own past so constantly before her. In his effort to protect the young woman from the specter, Captain Bostwick suffers Charlotte Marden's diffidence with greater patience than he otherwise might. Thus all the actions that take place outside the frame in which Mrs. Marden and Captain Bostwick hope to contain Sir Edmund Orme are determined to a great extent by their mutual act of framing, and thus of controlling, him.

To the developing allegorical reading of the ghost tales, this story adds the suggestion that the irreal has irrepressible power. It will signify in the real regardless of attempts to censor it or to devalue it. The representations, whether understood fully as Mrs. Marden does, or understood only partially and generally, as Captain Bostwick does, are nevertheless registered and become part of the fabric of reality by virtue of the reactions to it. James seems to be demonstrating the affective power of his secondhand representation of the fictive world. The felt impression has just as much persuasive power as a direct assault upon the senses, perhaps even more because it is so subtle, so uncertain, and therefore so ominous.

The remaining stories in this range of representation should, if James's efforts have not been in vain, be fairly easy to read by the reader now indoctrinated by, and practiced in referring to, the conceptual frame of the volume. "The Real Right Thing" and "The Jolly Corner" present other collusions of real and irreal. "The Real Right Thing" relates the refusal of the irreal to be reified in the real, whereas "The Jolly Corner" tells of an irreality so palpable that it becomes an alternate existence co-existent with the real. "The Real Right Thing" is the tale of a would-be biographer, George Withermore, who moves into his late subject's study at the behest of the subject's widow, only to be gradually possessed by his subject and as a result to honor his subject's wishes that no biography be written. In this odd twist to logic of "The Birthplace," the intrinsic expresses itself by refusing to be expressed: absence asserts itself and is made present only as a story about an absent signified's refusal to be reduced to a palpable sign. The real past is truly irrecoverable except as traces that are frequently dissimulating, because it has been lost through death to irreality. Even records of and from the past, such as the "diaries, letters, memoranda, notes, documents of many sorts" from which Withermore would mine biographical material, are displaced from the time they reflect, and these reflections are at best only questionably accurate, as James asserts in the preface:

> The habitual teller of tales finds these things [references to the past] in old note-books—which however but shifts the burden a step; since how, and under what inspiration, did they first wake up in these rude cradles? One's notes, as all writers remember, sometimes explicitly mention, sometimes indirectly reveal, and sometimes wholly dissimulate, such clues and such obligations. (17:xxi)

In conjunction with "Sir Edmund Orme," "The Real Right Thing" implies that if the irreal desires to be revealed it will make itself felt regardless of our best efforts to suppress it. If, however, the irreal is completely inaccessible, our best efforts will succeed at only suggesting what it may have been and therefore we will displace the real, right past (in this case) with an artificial image of it.

The preface prepares James's readers for this shifting focus of the conceptual frame. As James considers reviewing old notebooks, he realizes that these signs of the past are indeterminate. One noted germ, for example, may have become any one of several very different tales. In light of the finished products before him, James considers alternate courses of action: "we chance on some idea we *have* afterwards treated; then, greeting it with tenderness, we wonder at the first form of a motive that was to lead us so far and to show, no doubt, to eyes not our own, for so other; then we heave the deep sigh of relief over all that is never, thank goodness, to be done again. Would we have embarked on *that* stream had we known?—and what might n't we have made of this one *had n't* we known!" (17:xxi). Inaccessibility of the past, mirrored by the inaccessibility of the future (the mutual reflection of "The Birthplace" and "The Beast in the Jungle"), leads James to confront alternate histories that would have led to other presents. In this way, James transforms the coupling of the real and the intrinsic that has informed the entire volume into a frame for "The Jolly Corner."

Spencer Brydon, gravely pursuing the road not taken by prowling at night through the house in which he chose not to live and searching there for the self he chose not to become, is reminiscent— perhaps an inversion— of Morris Gedge seeking the divine Poet's presence in the birthplace. But Brydon confronts his alter ego, his alternative self, unlike the famous playwright of "The Private Life," Clare Vawdrey. The real pursues and confronts the irreal just as James has done throughout this volume and through his fanciful consideration of the results of aesthetic choices not made. Inherent in the author's reading of his tale are all the tales that James might have written had he made a different choice during the process of composition; "The Jolly Corner" suggests that we each contain usually buried alternative selves, representing alternate personal histories and alternate choices that were never made. These unlived lives and never-made choices are obliquely signified in the reality we have chosen to inhabit: our identity, based on choices we have made for ourselves, frames and is a text that both covers and signifies unrealized possibilities. Thus like a double helix, the irreal is attached to the real, the absence to the presence, the intrinsic to the extrinsic, at every point and at every moment. With this tale, then, James drops the philosophical into a lower register, one in which the reader can place him- or herself. James allows us to understand that process of relating reality and irreality as a process of chasing a ghost that is just as valid as the body that we see ourselves in. Another way of saying this is that James uses "The Jolly Corner" to demonstrate to the reader that art and world are parallel constructions, each equally valid and related in some essential way, just as the self we imagine and the self imagining are related.

"The Jolly Corner" ends this range of representation by raising the conceptual frame to a new, expansive plane that attributes value to one's knowledge of and desire for a union of what is and what is not. Alice Staverton, like the narrator of "The Private Life," has an Emersonian perspective that broadens in ever-increasing and inclusive circles; as her perspective broadens, antitheses are revealed as equivalencies. This is the broadest perspective possible in James's fiction; it allies reader and author and therefore satisfies James's overarching desire for an affinity with his audience. In "The Jolly Corner" this perspective results in true love and a million a year. The tale is framed by James's report that in spite of his expectations to the contrary, "The Jolly Corner" was simultaneously published in the New York Edition and, he says, "elsewhere only as I write" (xv): unlike "The Birthplace," "The Jolly Corner" has great intrinsic, aesthetic value and has demonstrated extrinsic value too. The latter may be figured by James as the dark, ominous other (and in "The Jolly Corner" as the *irreal* other), but it is recovered nevertheless as part and parcel of the work of art.

In the Third Range of Representation: The Misplaced or Replaced "Julia Bride"

Although James claims at the outset of his prefatory discussion of the last section, the isolate "Julia Bride," that this story is placed in volume 17 for material reasons only and that it is otherwise "quite out of [its] congruous company," the nature of value virtually explodes in "Julia Bride" onto the American social scene of turn-of-the-century New York. Moreover, the interplay of the real and the irreal that has characterized much of the volume becomes in "Julia Bride" part of the aesthetic of the narrative itself. James misleads the reader, however, from arriving at this conclusion by attempting to sever the last story's ties to the nine tales that precede it, and by emphasizing the ghostly "link" that "is with others yet to come" (17:xxv). "Julia Bride" does have more in common with works from James's later phase, particularly

The Ambassadors, The Wings of the Dove, and *The Golden Bowl,* in which the center of interest is "the achieved iridescence from within" the narratives, rather than with James's earlier works, in which "there are [occasionally] voluminous, gross and obvious ways of seeking that effect of the distinctly rich presentation" (17:xxv). Yet it does not represent a beginning point of the final phase; its very placement at the end of this volume rather than at the beginning of the next (perhaps in lieu of "Daisy Miller") suggests that in constructing the Edition James saw "Julia Bride" as a transitional piece, one that cloaks subject matter in "the mantle of iridescence naturally and logically . . . produced" by style (that is, subject is *signified* by style; 17:xxv).

James's dissimulation has the unexpected effect of enhancing Edition architecture. By linking "Julia Bride" to narratives yet to come, and specifically to "Daisy Miller," the first story in the next volume, James builds intervolume bridges that are based in this instance on social type (the American girl), authorial intention (rich presentation produced by iridescent narrative rather than through more obvious methods, such as recourse to blatant symbolism), and style. James claims that the tale will "suggest itself on the occasion of" our reading of the succeeding narratives in the Edition as if, like "The Altar of the Dead," "Julia Bride" were to be a prototype for those stories, or like Sir Edmund Orme, "Julia Bride" will hover in the margins of those tales when the reader of the Edition attends to them.

Suggesting a sense of unity and purpose for the New York Edition as he does (and James does so in other prefaces as well as in this one), James's denial of intertextual relations with the preceding tales is suspect. The explanation that "Julia Bride" is misplaced for "material reasons" cannot but recall the already resounding note of material value that has played throughout the preface and echoed in the tales. Furthermore, the author's desire to place like with like is here for the first time demonstrably mitigated by the limits of possibility, of which he spoke while yoking "Altar" and "Beast" in the first pages of the preface. Thus the story is framed by two pronounced deferences to material, practical concerns that themselves act as a parenthetic frame to the main body of the preface. Yoked to these acknowledgments of the material world is an attempted denial of the past— of the preceding tales—as if it were possible that the occasion of "Julia Bride," as James would have put it, could be a beginning unfettered by associations to the author's history. Misleading the reader to consider only the future possibilities and ramifications of "Julia Bride" (as one meets it while reading the New York Edition from beginning to end), James places the reader into the same compromising position as Julia Bride occupies. Her false belief that she can construct her future by first denying the past and then rewriting it leads to her social downfall. Especially since the volume has fostered a developing intertextual reading, the reader will hardly be able to bracket "Julia Bride" to the exclusion of the conceptual frame instigated by the preface.

As the tale's placement for "material reasons" suggests, strong ties do exist between "Julia Bride" and the tales preceding it. Questions of value are directed exclusively to the social scene. Julia Bride is "the silver key, tiny in itself, that . . . [unlocks] the treasure of a whole view of manners and morals, a whole range of American social aspects" (17:xxvi). In every circumstance she is the most beautiful woman, and she has grown accustomed to the admiration and deference of gentlemen. Her beauty and the prodigious social opportunities have a clear extrinsic value: six proposals of marriage. Her presumed prospect of a better return, however, results in six broken engagements. When she wins the attentions of Basil French, a devastatingly handsome, enormously wealthy, and socially elite bachelor, Julia first understands the negative influences that the past can have on the present. In this case, her value undermines itself: her extraordinary engagement record renders Julia Bride unmarriagable to Basil French. Her value has been compromised, in other words, by the very signs of her value. To further encumber her, James provides Julia Bride with a thrice-married mother whose liaisons have brought mother and daughter no closer to a permanent connection with monied society than have Julia's profound good looks. Beauty is a valuable commodity, but engaging in any trade—making any significant use of that beauty—that does not result in consummation of the deal, devalues it.

Awakening to this realization when it is nearly too late, Julia Bride decides that, rather than change her hopes for the future, she will revise history in order to satisfy her desires. She asks her first stepfather, Mr. Pitman, to tell Basil French that his divorce from Julia's mother was entirely a matter of his own villainy. Unfortunately for his stepdaughter, Mr. Pitman is himself about to marry and would rather not have misrepresentations of his character spread about town. Julia then asks an ex-fiancé, Murray Brush, to tell Basil French that there had been nothing of any significance between them— that her value had not been so great as to result in a *real* engagement. Brush furtively agrees. A moment too late Julia realizes that Brush would destroy her the instant the opportunity presented itself—not because he resents her implication that her past relation with him is completely subservient to her intended future with Basil French, but because such treachery, in the guise of a self-sacrificing warning, might ultimately win Basil French's gratitude.

Good looks, social connections, incomes, and good reputations have great extrinsic value in this American society: they all bring a good price at the marriage market. When Julia Bride finds that she has lost her reputation (much as Daisy Miller does, though Daisy never cares so much as Julia Bride does), and thereby lost the best chance she is ever likely to have at obtaining social connections and income, she realizes that her good looks are less valuable than she once believed. In spite of them, Basil French probably will not marry her and Murray Brush is willing to destroy her future to better his own.

James makes elusive value and its signification in the real world part of his aesthetic in "Julia Bride." James predicts that the plot will "prevail at best by indirectness," which is precisely the point made allegorically in the second range of representation (17:xxv). The tale presents the subject's reflections of events that happen off the page; all of these reflections are no more and no less than desires for greater personal value and are made in the context of Julia Bride's increasingly desperate awareness of her predicament. Making the main character's subjective consciousness the only register of plot changes what would normally be considered the real—the events of the real world—into the irreal because those events never occur directly but only as signs, as reverberations, in the subject's impressions. Yet as Laurence B. Holland argues throughout *Expense of Vision*,[16] displacement of plot onto the subject's registering consciousness does not devalue plot. In fact, such displacement enhances the value of plot by transforming it into irreal and intrinsic reflection of the world (and of the subject's consciousness itself), which is the nature of art. Moreover, what we have previously considered the irreal—the abstract, the removed, the represented, the supernatural—is made virtually real and very present as the substance of James's narrative. In "Sir Edmund Orme," Mrs. Marden's reaction to the ghost was the register of that ghost's existence. The ghost made its mark in reality by affecting her. In "Julia Bride," the realities of the social scene for a young woman who was not properly indoctrinated into the complex, rigid, and fiercely competitive mores of the game, are made real to the reader only as felt impressions, fears, insights, and "the perfect clearance of passion" (17:541). Concrete reality

---

16. Laurence Bedwell Holland, *The Expense of Vision: Essays on the Craft of Henry James* (Princeton: Princeton University Press, 1964).

irradiates through a mantle of irreality as if figure and ground have been reversed.

James brings his prefatory discussion of "Julia Bride" to a close only after emphasizing that all that has been said in this preface frame is a prelude to a reading of the ten tales as authorial performance. "Julia Bride" is really the author's "predicament" (17:xxviii), which James explains is "the consciousness, in that connexion, but of finding myself, after so many years astride the silver-shod, sober-paced, short-stepping, but oh so hugely nosing, so tenderly and yearningly and ruefully sniffing, grey mule of the 'few thousand words,' ridiculously back where I had started" (17:xxviii). After taking such pains to set up "Julia Bride" as the beginning of a new phase of the New York Edition, James finds that really, after all, he is once again talking about the *nouvelle*, a subject he has taken up earlier in this preface and in prefaces to preceding volumes. As Julia Bride learns, the past and future are bridged, and one inevitably returns to one's point of origins, as James has done so many times in these prefaces. What counts for James is the shadow he casts as he finds his way back to the beginning of things: implicit in his journey is consideration of what he has made of his art in the process. He clutches to the claim that his works have value, James confesses, "since I feel that without it the shadow I may have cast might n't bear comparison even with that of limping Don Quixote assisted through his castle-gate and showing but thankless bruises for laurels" (17:xxviii–xxix). Without believing that the intrinsic value he perceived in his art should be reflected in its extrinsic value, James would feel himself worthy only of the bruises he has received at the marketplace.

Imputed and borrowed are the natures of both intrinsic and extrinsic value. The extrinsic value of an object, including a literary manuscript, is imputed to it according to its success at the marketplace. The same value is borrowed from the exchange value in goods that it produces for the author, publisher, distributor, and others connected with its production, marketing, and ownership. The intrinsic value of art in particular is imputed to it by critics, for example, and these values, as Hans Robert Jauss argues, are diachronic, borrowed from both the literary work's relation to its genre and literary history (the traditions that frame it and in which it is therefore perceived and by which it is evaluated) and the historical moment in which the literary artwork appears. Thus, as Jauss claims, a work's supposedly intrinsic value may significantly change over time. What is "good" is not always eternal. Jauss implies that the very concept of value itself is intrinsic and absent.[17] Like the ghost of meaning, value slips from our grasp as soon as we fix upon it. It does not exist except by its impression in the world: these impressions are what constitutes the presence, though indirect, of value.

In this last reference to Don Quixote, moreover, James compares himself with a poor sensitive gentleman who lives in the shadowy areas between the real and the irreal, where neither realm is fully distinguishable from the other and where both enjoy active intercourse. There is value in the life that creates works of art even if those works are unappreciated by the public (as Don Quixote's actions were so often unappreciated). In the long run, however, Don Quixote brought about great intrinsic and extrinsic improvements in the lives that he touched, and he accomplished this by allowing the irreal—his dreams—to make their impression on his life and actions. So too would James, through his art—his "religion of doing"—which would eventually bring him the honor and readership he deserved. James knew this as Don Quixote did not, for James stood in the reader's place and understood that Quixote, though unappreciated in his own world, resides eternally in the context of a monumental narrative that fully appreciates him. In the New York Edition, James constructed a similar narrative context for his own authorial consciousness in the hopes of finding a reader like himself.

17. Jauss, *Aesthetic Experience*, chap. 1.

6

CONSCIOUSNESS AND THE
CONSTRUCTION OF IDENTITY

Reading The Portrait of a Lady *Through the Preface*

If the overarching goal of the New York Edition is to create modern readers who will appreciate James's work, and if the strategy for achieving that end is to canonize the author, making him the totem by which his readers will identify themselves, then the Edition must construct a clear and assessible identity for the author, one that will lend itself to both the indoctrinated readers and the novels and tales themselves. In short, through the prefaces James attempts to create the ideal modern author. James accomplishes this by making the entire New York Edition an elaborate construction of authorial consciousness, which James asserts in the beginning of the first preface, is precisely what "these notes represent" (1:v). In the preface to *The Portrait of a Lady*, James explains his logic, and it is a thoroughly modernist notion of the self. Consciousness provides a context by which one is identified, and therefore the elaboration of authorial consciousness is the articulation of identity. "Tell me what the artist is," James says, "and I will tell you of what he has *been* conscious" (3:xi). Consciousness supplies the determining frame of identity; whereas identity constitutes a text that signifies the history of the individual's consciousness. By telling us in the prefaces of what he as author has been conscious, James would indicate his identity as author, and this identity will extend itself both to the novels and tales by contextualizing them in the author's creating and consuming consciousness, and to the readers, who will assume it metonymically. As Barthes predicted, reading and writing become interrelated activities, all within the space of the frame where both are idealized.

Frequently in the prefaces, James refers to other writers and other works to offer those references as signs of the literary-historical, aesthetic, and sometimes critical contexts in which he, and by extension his works, are to be understood and identified. He is telling us, however, not only that of which he as author has been conscious; he is providing us with a list of contextual icons of which we as ideal readers will also be conscious, using them as guideposts in our assumption of the Jamesian identity. While writing *Roderick Hudson*, for instance, James says that initially he was "nestled, technically, in those days, and with yearning, in the great shadow of Balzac; his august example . . . towered for [him] over the scene," both the one in which he wrote, and the one that in writing, he made (1:xi). And again, in the preface to *The American*, James says that the "full artistic consciousness" is "inevitably expressing himself, under the influence of one value or the other" and then names Scott, Balzac, and Zola as the "men of largest responding imagination before the human scene" of which he writes (2:xiv). Literary references such as these name the icons of authorial consciousness. They identify the primary determinants of authorial identity (James was a writer in the shadows of late Romanticism, Realism, and early Naturalism) and textual identity (*The American*, while betraying a few stray Romantic filaments, is primarily a Realist text, according to James).[1] James is consciously constructing methodological and literary historical contexts for the novels. Yet these contexts are imputed to authorial consciousness as it was operative at the time of writing. James was aware of Balzac when he wrote *Roderick Hudson*; he was conscious of the aesthetic values represented by Scott, Balzac, and Zola and of his need to make choices among them.

Following J. Hillis Miller's relation of repetition and authority, we might put it this way: James had either to gain his validity as a novelist by following in the path already begun by someone he honors (or honored), and thus invoke Platonic repetition, which focuses on affiliation as a means of empowerment; or he had to repudiate all prior aesthetics and invoke Nietzschean repetition, which focuses on difference as a means of empowerment. Throughout the prefaces, James makes no claims to absolute originality and so rejects the Nietzschean mode in favor of the Platonic insofar as

---

1. Authorial identity and textual identity are distinguished because they may differ in the New York Edition to the extent that the early works, in spite of their revision, sometimes offer a glimpse into an earlier, slightly different authorial identity than the one that James concocts in the present moment of his preface writing.

he is concerned with the writers who have influenced him. In fact, he refers and defers to well-known models in an effort to bolster his claims of value for the text and for the artist who authored it *because* he has acknowledged that identity depends upon consciousness, which is the context one provides for oneself (or which is otherwise provided). Presumably, these relations make his own work more collectible.

James is not admitting derivation so much as he is identifying the literary values that he has assumed from various writers over the years. In *The Book World of Henry James*, Adeline Tintner argues, in fact, that James's "devouring interest in [others'] fiction lay in measuring his mind against the works of others and that his pleasure arose from rewriting them in his own way." He was an inveterate collector of impressions, which he took from the novels he read and the novelists with whom he associated. James's own statement about the aggressiveness of his reading supports this contention: "To read a novel at all," James wrote to H. G. Wells, "I perform afresh, to my sense, the act of writing it, that is of rehandling the subject accordingly to my own lights and over-scoring the author's form and pressure with my own vision and understanding." Like the wind-blown seed of a good story and like the historical facts found by a seeking fabulist, the works that he reads are collected by James and subjected to his authorial imagination. The result is sometimes the origin of a new work by James, and sometimes an addition, if only a reference, in a work that otherwise has no relation to the collected text. Tintner concludes from her study of these intertextual references that the reason James refers to the works of Shakespeare, Milton, and most especially Balzac, for example, is not to make a show of his readerly and writerly possession of those authors. Throughout his fiction, James alludes to their works to create an analogic matrix by which his novels and tales might be illuminated. Such a system relies on "a careful and ingenious system of recall"—on a reader who can discover the signified source texts as well as Tintner does.[2] The literary-historical contexts provided in the prefaces, then, are to become that of which the reader is conscious as he or she reads the prefaced narrative. The result, James hopes, will be a deeper and more meaningful appreciation of his accomplishments that will in turn produce a more finely indoctrinated reader. Henry James, the inveterate collector, in other words, has his sights on the reader too.

---

2. Tintner argues, however, that this system does not construct identity: "it provides an extension of, not an identification with, the classic model." Adeline Tintner, *The Book World of Henry James: Appropriating the Classics* (Ann Arbor: UMI Research Press, 1987), xix, xxi.

In this sense, the eighteen prefaces construct affiliation between the reader and the world of Henry James as it is registered in authorial consciousness, which, as a consequence of the reader's acquired consciousness of it, will reconstruct the reader's identity. Affiliation is accomplished, however, preface by preface. The preface to *Roderick Hudson* induces a reading of that novel that accounts for the towering shadow cast by Balzac. James's ideal reader must account for that shadow too, as Tintner has done. Each preface contextualizes the prefaced novel by selecting and representing icons that provide identity peculiar to that novel yet which gesture toward the author as he reads and recalls the writing of the prefaced text. The preface to *The Portrait of a Lady* is a classic case. Laurence Holland argues that in the preface to *The Portrait of a Lady*, James is actively involved in the process of self-creation. The preface's "full relevance to the *Portrait*, and its brilliance as an essay in its own right, come to light only when read with full attention to its metaphorical details and to the intimate drama which moves implicitly within the more explicit argument." By turning his attention to the subtext that is alluded to in the rhetoric of the preface and implied by the terms and tropes of its argument, Holland discovers that the preface is "a conscience-stricken inquiry into the deepest implications of James's craft," instigated by James's "direct confrontation of his imaginative work" while preparing revisions for the New York Edition. Holland concludes that the preface expresses a process of self-definition—of framing an identity—"for the artist . . . [that] is central to the novel itself."[3] In *Portrait*'s preface, James attempts to affiliate the reader with him by leading the reader through the semiotic field of authorial identity. The icons in this field include other writers, the Italian landscape, and even characters from the novel itself. James wants the reader to perceive in the novel its true origin, the actual source of its power: the author. His strategy in this instance is to portray the text as a semiotic field that is, like its author's consciousness, permeable.

The preface to *The Portrait of a Lady* suggests that the identity of the narrative, like that of the author, is determined by the literary "objects" that James (re)collects as he wrote, read and, presumably, revised the text. The preface to *Portrait* begins by selectively organizing elements from the scene of writing and making them contribute to the novel's identity. James claims that the Italian scene was essential to the compositional process:

---

3. Laurence Bedwell Holland, *The Expense of Vision: Essays on the Craft of Henry James* (Princeton: Princeton University Press, 1964), 3.

I had rooms on Riva Schiavoni, at the top of a house near the passage leading off to San Zaccaria; the waterside life, the wondrous lagoon spread before me, and the ceaseless human chatter of Venice came in at my windows, to which I seem to myself to have been constantly driven, in the fruitless fidget of composition, as if to see whether, out in the blue channel, the ship of some right suggestion, of some better phrase, of the next happy twist of my subject, the next true touch for my canvas, might n't come into sight. (3:v)

Recollection of the inspirations and distractions of the Venetian scene establish a referential relation between the internal world of James's study and the external, though aestheticized, world of Italy. Through the agency of authorial consciousness, the rich human scene inflates the text, gives it substance and direction. Yet according to this passage, the particularities of that scene are signified most fully by what James refers to as the architecture of the novel: its style, the narrative pace, and the other elements of fiction that James believed formed his essential relationship with the reader. As we saw earlier in the discussion of narrative origins, however, James altered the history of *The Portrait of a Lady* slightly but significantly by setting its origin in Italy rather than in the obscure past alluded to but never described in his notebooks. The preface, then, does not reveal a true identity of the novel by revealing what the author was actually conscious of when he began writing; it creates a desired identity for *Portrait* that is completely controlled by James's circumspect consciousness at the time of writing the preface.

James's choice of an Old World origin implicates a prevailing theme of *Portrait* and in the life and consciousness of the author: the contrast of the Old World and the New. Sandra Djwa notes that "James, like Nathaniel Hawthorne before him, found innocence and nature in the New World garden, but not art. It was to the Old World, especially Italy, the world of the court and of 'lords' and 'ladies' (and their artistic representations) that one must go for a knowledge of good and evil and thus a fully developed consciousness."[4] And like so much else in the prefaces, this tale of origin compliments James's aesthetic: knowledge of good and evil is intricately bound up in aesthetic experience. To write a novel of consciousness, James had to look to the European scene; only there could he be assured of

4. Sandra Djwa, "*Ut Pictura Poesis*: The Making of a Lady," *Henry James Review* 7, nos. 2–3 (1986): 72.

finding the moral complexities of aesthetic consciousness that his narrative required. Appreciation of aesthetic richness is a prerequisite of his
subject's imagination; to James, experience of art *is* experience of life.
Christof Wegelin argues correctly that the "ultimate good in James's view
of things . . . is the awareness which results from the full life"—awareness,
in this instance, of the moral complexities, which heavily contribute to the
developing consciousness. However, Wegelin asserts, "Art and life are in
James's view of things . . . closely related, 'the house of life and the palace
of art,' as James recalls in *Small Boy and Others*, became at an early time
too 'mixed and interchangeable' to allow so simple an opposition between
moral and aesthetic values."[5] To make consciousness both the primary
vehicle of narrative and its object, James was obliged to turn from the
safety of the New World, from the innocence of a culture whose aesthetic
vision and iconography was not yet fully developed, and set his innocent
American subject against the iconographically rich European scene. *Portrait*'s Henrietta Stackpole offers a caricature of the simplicity and naïveté
of the American aesthetic experience in the nineteenth century; she ex-
emplifies the aesthetic hazards of New World life. Her lack of appreciation for art and her inability to distinguish ornaments from icons are
demonstrated when she mistakes a necklace worn by one of Lord Warburton's sisters as a symbol of aristocracy rather than as an object of profound beauty and sentimental value. Her rustic interpretation can be attributed to America's persistent infatuation with Romanticism in the age
of European Realism. In his biography of Hawthorne, James comments on
the reliance of American Romantic novelists (Hawthorne and Cooper, in
particular) on simplistic, obvious symbols and melodramatic contortions
of plot—the terms of Henrietta's experience of the world. These characteristics of American Romanticism inform the aesthetic sensibility that
James chose to abandon in favor of the more complex and, therefore, the
morally "dangerous" aesthetic vision of Europe. Only in the Old World
could James hope for an interchange between subject and cultural context that would produce both an acutely perceptive consciousness and a
world worthy of being its object. Only in the Old World, moreover, could
he develop a consciousness suitable to the quality of authorship to which
he aspired.

5. Christof Wegelin, "The American as a Young Lady," in *Twentieth-Century Interpretations
of The Portrait of a Lady: A Collection of Critical Essays*, ed. Peter Buitenhuis (Englewood Cliffs,
N.J.: Prentice Hall, 1968), 59, 58.

The subtleties of the relation of author and text are implicated here. As the inveterate collector of impressions, James consumed the "waterside life" and "the ceaseless human chatter of Venice," then transformed and re-created them in his fiction, as if fiction were constructed of objects found in the world and taken by the author to his study (the preface's objective correlative of the artist's imagination, which is itself constantly infiltrated by the cultural context in which it is located) where the collected objects are transformed into the author's work of art. Yet even if the individual cannot, the author must always control his or her consciousness and the impressions made thereon. The superabundance of "romantic and historic sites," James says, "such as the land of Italy abounds in" and other external sources of inspiration threatened the tenuous balance between self-determination and determinism that Isabel Archer is never able to achieve but upon which James's art depends. They threatened to overwhelm and to displace the narrative because they threaten to overwhelm authorial consciousness; "they are too rich in their own life and too charged with their own meanings" to be allowed free reign of the artist's imagination (3:v). James suggests that freedom to choose a context for the work of art, as for the self, does not imply freedom from, but instead depends upon, determination by context. That is why James finds it imperative that he control the variants that provide context for the narrative.

Identifying the impressions made on him by the land in which he would have writing begin, James seems to be setting the scene for his naming of the story's origin. Yet he continually defers the naming of the germ or seed, focusing instead on his authorship of the text and then on the literary traditions that influenced him. In lieu of the authority of origins, which had become problematic because James had suppressed one version of the origin and promoted another, James relies on the authority of origination. He describes "the usual origin of the fictive picture," citing Ivan Turgenev as both authority and subject (3:vii):

> it began for him almost always with the vision of some person or persons, who hovered before him, soliciting him, as the active or passive figure, interesting him and appealing to him just as they were and by what they were. He . . . then had to find for them the right relations, those that would most bring them out; to imagine, to invent and select and piece together the situations most useful and favourable to the sense of the creatures themselves, the complications they would be most likely to produce and to feel. (3:vii)

Turgenev began with character, really a character type without connections to any predetermined plot. Plot, he believed, is inherent in character just as the mature plant is predicted by the seed. Such is the story James later relates about the genesis of Isabel Archer's narrative, and his deference to Turgenev establishes a useful precedent that will later validate James's sui generis approach to Isabel's origin. Perhaps at the early stage of his preface writing for the New York Edition, James felt that his own aesthetic choices of subject, particularly his location of interest in the consciousness of a young woman, were not easily defensible on logical or aesthetic grounds. His invocation of Turgenev, the established master, may also suggest that James's method of authorship is his claim to the readership that would idolize Turgenev. And in fact James continues by transforming his reminiscence of Turgenev's comments into actual attributed speech, enabling Turgenev's voice to contribute to the accumulating identity of the author and to lend the Russian novelist's dignity and magnificence as a novelist to James's aesthetic of fiction—his focus on the impressions of his protagonist's consciousness:

> "To arrive at these things is to arrive at my 'story,' " he [Turgenev] said, "and that's the way I look for it. The result is that I'm often accused of not having 'story' enough. I seem to myself to have as much as I need—to show my people, to exhibit their relations with each other; for that is all my measure. . . . As for the origin of one's wind-blown germs themselves, who shall say, as you ask, where *they* come from? We have to go too far back, too far behind, to say. . . . They accumulate, and we are always picking them over, selecting among them. . . . They are so, in a manner prescribed and imposed—floated into our minds by the current of life." (3:vii–viii)

At the same time, James is able to deflect criticism of his own work by diverting it to Turgenev and then allowing Turgenev to man the defense.

After James relies on Turgenev to articulate a theory of narrative origins, he summons Shakespeare and George Eliot to defend his choice of a young woman as subject. "The Isabel Archers, and even much smaller female fry, insist on mattering," James contends (3:xiii). Citing Hetty Sorrel, Maggie Tulliver, Rosamond Vincy, Gwendolen Harleth, Portia, and Juliet, James identifies his heroine by identifying her peers. Rather than historicize his narrative to enhance the value of its subject, as Hawthorne has done, James builds his house of fiction in a posh neighborhood. And in similar fashion he elevates his critical and aesthetic views by expressing them as forms of quotation. He quotes Turgenev rather than deduce principle through analysis. Later in the preface he quotes George Eliot on the great role played by the "frail vessels" who are otherwise so frequently overlooked as subjects of art: "George Eliot has admirably noted it—'In these frail vessels is borne onward through the ages the treasure of human affection.'" (3:xiii). James might very well have been quoting her on the novel itself.

James carefully affiliates his heroine and her story with others that have already been adjudged among the best just as he earlier affiliated himself with Turgenev. James's reliance on others for authority and value, and indeed his acts of ventriloquism, bespeak the common intertextual condition of all discourse: as Lawrence Danson claims, "signs refer to other signs, that language is in effect always quotation."[6] Because language is always referential, it is always derivative (signs derive meaning from signifieds). Originality, therefore, is an ideal that is always absent, and can never exist in or be discovered through discourse. Originality is signified only by our awareness of repetition, which tries to substitute for originality in its absence. Julia Kristeva writes in this regard that "each word (text) is an intersection of words (texts) where at least one other word (text) can be read," claiming, as James implies, that narrative is the intersection of impressions of the subjective consciousness, of authorial consciousness, and of the reader's consciousness of the text, as each consciousness is eternally quoting the others.[7] Authority in discourse must accommodate this condition of discourse that Danson and Kristeva describe. The preface's displacement of the old beginning of the novel mentioned in James's notebooks, for example, reenacts the sacrifice of originality for composition, for the arrangement of signs into a complex narrative structure that acquires meaning rather than assumes some preexistent meaning.

James has elected to compose authorial and aesthetic identity by following the Platonic mode of repetition, in which identity is derived from external sources which are eventually made internal. To enable his reader to follow suit, James cites selected literary precedents in order to have his reader internalize the aesthetic value systems that he has internalized from his reading and that his work embodies. The selectivity of the process cannot be

---

6. Lawrence Danson, *Max Beerbohm and the Act of Writing* (Oxford: Clarendon Press, 1989), 431.

7. Kristeva asserts that "every signifying practice is a field of transpositions of various signifying systems (an inter-textuality)." *Revolution in Poetic Language*, trans. Margaret Waller (New York: Columbia University Press, 1984), 66.

overlooked. James never conceived of the prefaces as frames of exhaustive reference; he articulates references that best meet his desire for an ideal reader. Even the quantity of carefully selected references is thoughtfully controlled. For example, by referring to Turgenev, Shakespeare, and Eliot (and briefly to Dickens, Scott, and Stevenson) rather than to only one of them, James contextualizes his work with a conceptual frame of reference. James might have attributed the speech he invented for Turgenev to Eliot, for example, and not included Portia and Juliet on his list of young heroines who insist on mattering. Were James to attribute his novel to George Eliot's work in this way, then Eliot's work would be the sole pre-texts for *Portrait*; we would look to Eliot's aesthetic as a determining standard against which we might judge James's achievement. Such a marriage would devastate James's individual aesthetic and render him, like one of his characters, a signifier of another's authorial powers rather than a participant in, and contributor to, the realist aesthetic. To be composed amid a complex arrangement of con-textualizing elements does not subsume the self to any specific other. James implies that his work is the intersection—perhaps even the culmination—of these other writers and traditions. In addition, citing specific precedents and authorities allows James to suppress other potentially identifying but unde-sirable contexts, such as the American literary history of which *The Portrait of a Lady* is inevitably a part and apart. He does not mention Hawthorne, for example, whose novels and tales might suggest prototypes for Isabel Archer.

These selected references to James's writing and reading inevitably but implicitly locate origin, such as it is, in authorial consciousness, where the selection process takes place. Authorial consciousness contains intratextual references as well. Isabel Archer herself crosses the border from narrative to preface and stands as a mute icon, signifying her own oblique origin and attesting to the principle espoused by Turgenev that plot is inherent in character. Isabel's inherent plot, however, is a tale of possession: everyone in the novel seems to make a claim on Isabel, and James even allows some of these characters to cross the textual border in pursuit of her. It is in their exchange with the author that plot begins. James claims that after a restless night spent fretting over his heroine's fate and the almost certainly fragile narrative structure she would support, a small group of characters came to him with a solution. James locates the origin of this fictive picture, that is, in the author's imagination:

> I . . . waked up . . . in possession of them—of Ralph Touchett and
> his parents, of Madame Merle, of Gilbert Osmond and his daughter

and his sister, of Lord Warburton, Caspar Goodwood and Miss Stack-pole. . . . It was as if they had simply, by an impulse of their own, floated into my ken, and all in response to my primary question: "Well, what will she *do*?" Their answer seemed to be that if I would trust them they would show me; on which, with an urgent appeal to them to make it at least as interesting as they could, I trusted them. They were like the group of attendants and entertainers who come down by train when people in the country give a party; they represented the contract for carrying the party on. (3:xvii)

These characters collect Isabel into their plot, hoping that her presence would make it appreciable and therefore that her narrative value would reflect on them. James works with similar motives in his very construction of this exchange: "I seem to myself to have waked up one morning *in possession*" of these characters, he claims (3:xvii; emphasis added). He has collected them within this frame of his authorial identity, just as he previously collected Turgenev, Shakespeare, and George Eliot. They come from within the narrative yet are made temporally and physically antecedent: they are made part of the tale of origin and they are given presence in the preface. The result is at least an illusion of their extraliterary existence. Yet they never exist outside authorial consciousness: their first register in the world is in James's imagination, after he has already taken possession of them. They lend whatever significance they have to his authorial capacity. The ado they make out of (and for) Isabel Archer is similarly a sign of James's authorial power. The transference of the responsibility for plot from the author to the characters appurtenant to the initially isolated character of Isabel Archer is not abdication by the author but an institution of an aesthetic chain of being. The author appears to allow others to perform actions that are otherwise solely the author's to perform himself or to assign. By releasing Isabel Archer to Ralph Touchett and the others of her history, James brings those others under his purview. Entrusting them with his responsibility, he enlists them in his service as delegates or ambassadors.

Authorial power, however, is circumscribed by the necessity to choose a context by which one will be identified. As *The Portrait of a Lady* demonstrates, illusions of utter self-determination will result in the complete and irrevocable collection of the self by the more forceful imagination of another who knows the realities and strategies of contextualization. Such is the fate of Isabel Archer, who is collected in the prefaced narrative by her husband, and in the preface by her fellow characters and ultimately by her author.

The novel that James contextualizes by these richly allusive intertextual references is itself fraught with concerns for identity and self-determination in the face of the determining realities of context.

Isabel Archer's inculcated Emersonian belief in the possibility of total self-determination is countered by everyone in the novel, including the most stereotypically American of James's characters, Henrietta Stackpole. Chastising Isabel, Henrietta exclaims, " 'You can't always please yourself. You must sometimes please other people' " (3:310). And Madame Merle is the great champion of determination by context. She tells Isabel that " 'every human being has his shell and that you must take the shell into account. By the shell I mean the whole envelope of circumstances. There's no such thing as an isolated man or woman; we're each of us made up of some cluster of appurtenances. What shall we call our "self"? Where does it begin? where does it end? It overflows into everything that belongs to us—and then flows back again' " (3:287). To a limited extent, the "cluster of appurtenances" that identifies the self can be meticulously chosen and composed, but the interaction between it and the human being in possession is ineradicable, and the consequences of those choices are frequently lifelong. Unfortunately, when Isabel first comes to Europe, she does not heed these warnings.

Isabel's edenic Americanism is first questioned after she bids her American relatives farewell for the last time in her single life. "She has never had a keener sense of freedom, of the absolute boldness and wantonness of liberty, than when she turned away from the platform at the Euston Station on one of the last days of November, after the departure of the train that was to convey poor Lily, her husband and her children to their ship at Liverpool" (4:35). Isabel believes that the old beginning is suppressed and that her new life in the Old World is finally and absolutely under way without distressing ties to her young life in America. She believes herself, in other words, self-reliant. James indicates Isabel's blindness to the moral implications of her new circumstances by his critical allusion to Milton's *Paradise Lost*: "The world lay before her—she could do whatever she chose" (4:36). To a great extent, this intertextual reference redefines Isabel by suggesting that she has entered the fallen world (though she had done that when she first entered Gardencourt) and can no longer be understood as a being who naturally resides in Eden. Furthermore, the allusion suggests that Isabel herself is now fallen; like Adam and Eve she cannot do whatever she chooses. Most important, she can never again return to the Edenic state, whether or not she ever returns to America. Her belief in self-determination, therefore, has led her from a world in which her conceived self might have existed (though in a state of unconciousness); and it has brought her to a world in which that same conceived self cannot possibly exist, a fact of which she will become painfully aware as her marriage wears on. Isabel experiences wanton liberty because she has shed the one restricting context—her family—that she has ever known. Paradoxically, these are the first pangs of the realization that she cannot create her self, she cannot establish her own identity independent of several other defining, determining contexts in which she is helplessly trapped.

This is the lesson Madame Merle alludes to when she tells Isabel that American women are more adaptable to European culture than American men because "a woman . . . has no natural place anywhere; wherever she finds herself she has to remain on the surface and, more or less, to crawl" (3:280). Madame Merle implies that there are several determining factors, like gender, over which one has no control and yet to which one is always subject. Women are "mere parasites, crawling over the surface," Madame Merle claims; "we have n't our feet in the soil" (3:280). A woman has no "natural place" and consequently, as Madame Merle later explains, no natural identity. Madame Merle espouses a belief that gender is the rudimentary determinant of identity. For a woman, gender determines an identity that is paradoxically indeterminate: it limits the possibilities of a fully formed self. Perhaps this is why James would defend his "frail vessel" as a consciousness adequate to the task of carrying the narrative yet does not allow her to determine the plot—he turns her over to Ralph Touchett and the other co-conspirators who will determine Isabel's role for her.

Gender, like origins, is "antecedent to choice," as Ralph Touchett informs Henrietta Stackpole (3:125). Unlike gender, however, the origins of the self that is presented to the world are mutable, as James has shown in the preface. At her first encounter with Isabel, for example, Madame Merle speaks French so naturally that Isabel concludes that she must be a native Frenchwoman. Nevertheless, when Madame Merle admits her American heritage, Isabel, rather than registering disappointment, decides that "rarer even than to be French seemed it to be American on such interesting terms" as this thoroughly Europeanized compatriot (3:246). But eventually Madame Merle corrects her young companion's romantic idealization of the resident-alien status of Americans in Europe. She explains that suppression of one determinant of identity does not guarantee successful creation or adoption of another: "If we're not good Americans we're certainly poor Europeans," she says of her fellow expatriates (3:280). According to Madame Merle, one might disguise one's original identity, but one cannot easily become what one is not. From Isabel's initial, American perspective, these are excessive limits to self-determination that she does not accept until her own experience in Europe has sadly taught her otherwise.

In the novel, marriage for a woman is concomitant to the author's choosing a single writer or work with which to contextualize his work. It provides a very specific and determining context for a woman, who, as Madame Merle instructed Isabel, has no other real determinant. The more thoroughly entrenched a man is in his context, the more thoroughly his wife will be defined by it. Were Isabel to marry Caspar Goodwood, her life would be abundantly American. Nationality and marriage would determine her fate, and consequently she would experience "a diminished liberty" to determine her identity (3:162). The logic behind Henrietta Stackpole's insistence that Isabel marry Goodwood is precisely this: she wants Isabel to be thoroughly American. Henrietta's national chauvinism repeatedly expresses itself in her belief that no individual could aspire to a greater identity. Were Isabel to marry Lord Warburton, she would become a resident alien who is thoroughly involved in the British aristocracy of the late Victorian era. She would not contribute to Warburton's identity, for she has nothing that will increase his value in society; she would, however, be entirely subsumed by the role in which she would be inevitably cast. Isabel seems to understand the ramifications of a marriage alliance. When Lord Warburton asks her why she refuses his proposal, Isabel explains,

> "It's that I can't escape my fate."
>
> "Your fate?"
>
> "I should try to escape it if I were to marry you."
>
> "I don't understand. Why should not *that* be your fate as well as anything else?"
>
> "Because it's not," said Isabel femininely. "I know it's not. It's not my fate to give up—I know it can't be."
>
> Poor Lord Warburton stared, an interrogative point in either eye. "Do you call marrying *me* giving up?"
>
> "Not in the usual sense. It's getting—getting—getting a great deal. But it's giving up other chances."
>
> "Other chances for what?"
>
> "I don't mean chances to marry," said Isabel, her colour quickly coming back to her. And then she stopped, looking down with a deep frown, as if it were hopeless to attempt to make her meaning clear.

"I don't think it presumptuous in me to suggest that you'll gain more than you'll lose," her companion observed.

"I can't escape unhappiness," said Isabel. "In marrying you I shall be trying to." (3:184)

For Isabel, choosing to marry is to choose an identity that is determined by extrinsic qualities. To Isabel's way of thinking, marriage constitutes giving up the will to be self-determining; this is what Isabel means when she says marriage would be an attempt to escape her fate. By marrying before she has experienced enough of the world to develop a full consciousness, Isabel would be foresaking self-determination. She would be donning the garments—gathering about her the appurtenances—of a prefabricated destiny. Thus to marry Warburton, or Goodwood for that matter, would be a denial of responsibility for herself, an act Isabel finds morally indefensible. Of course the choice to marry, and the consequent choice of context, is largely self-determining, but like the choice to write, it is a choice of self-sacrifice.

Thus Isabel's marriage to Osmond mystifies nearly everyone who knows her, but she repeatedly explains what she has learned during her years of traveling the European continent, that self-determination is ultimately limited to one's choice of a determining context. She is making the inevitable choice that James made when he elected to affiliate himself with a specific literary tradition rather that to attempt complete originality. For a woman, however, affiliation is objectifying and ultimately defacing. After a year or two of traveling through Europe, Isabel had grown weary, "not of the act of living, but of that of observing"—of being an alien in every context. Osmond seems to offer a promise of an edifying context, and he allows Isabel the relative comfort of being observed without the effort required of reciprocity. And Isabel's weariness of being an active, perceiving consciousness allows her to deface herself, to suppress her strong will and desire for self-determination. She wants to serve Osmond's aesthetic cause, to provide him with the means to procure the identity for himself that, in reality, no fury of collecting could ever fully determine. Significantly, Isabel and Osmond meet in Italy: "Italy had been a party to their first impressions of each other"; therefore their initial perceptions of each other are greatly determined by the aesthetically rich and morally complex Italian landscape—a landscape, James warns in the preface, that tends to overshadow and envelop that which is placed in its context with its own luxuriant meanings. In this ambiguous air the two are able to misrepresent themselves and to misread each other.

Weary of ceaseless efforts at self-determination, Isabel marries Osmond, then, because she believes that he, of all the men she has met, has the highest aesthetic sense. He will make of her something great because, as his wife, she will be an icon signifying *his* greatness. Her social contiguity to her husband will in turn provide the all-important context in which his aesthetic greatness will be appreciated, and this will determine her identity and value as an element of that composition. Isabel's error is to confuse great aesthetic sensitivity with high moral sense. She has experienced Europe but she has not become European: her American idealism and naïveté still influence her judgment. Ralph Touchett, on the other hand, fully understands Osmond's need for power and its manifestation in his aesthetic sensibility. Ralph "recognized Osmond":

> He saw how he kept all things within limits; how he adjusted, reg-
> ulated, animated [his family's] manner of life. Osmond was in his
> element; at last he had material to work with. He always had an eye to
> effect, and his effects were deeply calculated. They were produced by
> no vulgar means, but the motive was as vulgar as the art was great. . . .
> His ambition was not to please the world, but to please himself by
> exciting the world's curiosity and then declining to satisfy it. . . . The
> thing he had done in his life most directly to please himself was his
> marrying Miss Archer; though in this case indeed the gullible world
> was in a manner embodied in poor Isabel, who had been mystified
> to the top of her bent. (4:144–45)

Both men recognize that Isabel Archer has the potential to signify a great aesthetic achievement. Ralph at least desires that through a very eventful, successful "career" as an American heiress in Europe, Isabel will realize that achievement as her own (though it will be bankrolled by him). Osmond, on the other hand, desires that she become the greatest of his self-referential icons. Unfortunately, before her marriage Isabel is too preoccupied with determining her own destiny to learn to read the signs scattered about her. And with Osmond, she is too concerned with suppression of her own personality to fully appreciate the significance of his life, habits, ideas, and surroundings. Only when her marriage begins to sour, when she has had ample opportunity to witness the greatest of the novel's connoisseurs in action, does Isabel finally begin to read her surroundings and interpret them correctly.

Once again Madame Merle plays a pivotal role in Isabel's destiny. Entering her house Isabel beholds Osmond and Madame Merle in conversation. "The impression had, in strictness, nothing unprecedented; but she felt it as something new, and the soundlessness of her step gave her time to take in the scene before she interrupted it." When she "perceived that they had arrived at a desultory pause in their exchange of ideas and were musing, face to face, with the freedom of old friends who sometimes exchange ideas without uttering them," Isabel receives an impression that changes her consciousness of Madame Merle, of her husband, and most dramatically of all, of herself: "the thing made an image, lasting only a moment, like a sudden flicker of light. Their relative positions, their absorbed mutual gaze, struck her as something detected" (4:164–65). With no information more specific than this, Isabel begins to unravel the history of deceptions that have brought her into such an unhappy marriage. Isabel learns to read for moral complexity. She understands that every work and action is the location of another word and action; that human lives are intertextual in a very real and sometimes imposing sense; that the multiplicity of meaning is a condition of the fallen world in which she now lives. She will never again assume that beauty and consciousness of the beautiful are equated with goodness and the desire to be good.

In sharp contrast to the texts and authors that James carefully admits into his frame of reference, Madame Merle, like an interloping text, has spoken in Isabel's life, but without Isabel's knowledge and approval. Pansy's mother constructs an excessively determining context into which Isabel will be placed and by which she will finally be judged, and therefore Madame Merle robs Isabel of the one real act of self-determination: the knowledgable choice of determining context-by-marriage. Nevertheless, Isabel concludes as James has, that although one may not be fully responsible for the events of one's destiny, one is always responsible for what one makes of one's life. That is to say, Isabel cannot help the machinations and devious plotting of those who would control her in a self-serving narrative of their own design, just as she cannot control the ado created for her by the characters that apprehend her in the preface. She is, however, responsible for the choices she has made, for the beliefs she holds, for her perceptions and interpretations of the world, and ultimately for the associations she forms with the world. She may allow others to determine aspects of her life, and she may defer to the judgments of others; however, those to whom she chooses to surrender her authority, those to whom she chooses to defer, and the attitude she will take toward her destiny are all expressions of the boundless freedom of the subjective consciousness. From the very title, James has made Isabel an art object because she is a woman; *Portrait* relates Isabel Archer's growing awareness of the moral complexity that such an existence requires.

The novel, its heroine, and its author have similar histories that implicate American innocence in their European fates. Their old beginnings in the New World are abandoned for new ones in the Old World, where consciousness can flourish in its recognition of Europe's two faces of Moral Complexity and Art. The preface to this novel of consciousness, therefore, implicates the aesthetic life in the struggle between good and evil that it dramatizes. This conjunction of moral and aesthetic values distinguishes *Portrait* from *The American,* James's earlier novel about an American abroad. The 1906 Isabel Archer is not "a female Newman" as James called the 1881 Isabel in a letter to William Dean Howells (*Letters* 2:72). She becomes too thoroughly Europeanized—her worldview becomes too thoroughly aesthetic—to resemble Newman. Isabel Archer sails from America, however, like Christopher Newman, a doctrinally pure Emersonian idealist, believing that self-reliance is self-creation, who learns as she crosses and recrosses the European landscape that her American Romanticism blinded her to the complicated and enmeshed circumstances into which she entered when she first stepped over the threshold of Gardencourt. As Richard Poirier claims, the innocent logic of Isabel's New World transcendentalism eventually "takes its vengeance" on her.[8]

If Isabel is an aesthetic object to be collected, *Portrait* offers several examples of American men living in Europe who, reminiscent of James at his study window in Venice, attempt self-determination by collecting. They make appurtenant to themselves self-determining icons that bespeak the experience and value of the Old World, for example. Yet, as Madame Merle explains, these icons are inadequate masks covering the lack of identity from which these men suffer: " 'Mr. Ralph Touchett: an American who lives in Europe.' That signifies absolutely nothing—it's impossible anything should signify less. 'He's very cultivated,' they say: 'he has a very pretty collection

---

8. "Drama in *The Portrait of a Lady,*" in *Twentieth Century Interpretations of The Portrait of a Lady: A Collection of Critical Essays,* ed. Peter Buitenhuis (Englewood Cliffs, N.J.: Prentice Hall, 1968), 35. Leon Edel says James felt "that Emerson represented American innocence and naiveté, only half-understanding that the tree in Eden had offered not only knowledge of evil but access to the world's wisdom." *Henry James: The Middle Years, 1884–94* (London: Rupert Hart-David, 1963), 174.

of old snuff-boxes.' The collection is all that's wanted to make it pitiful"
(3:280–82). Gilbert Osmond, another expatriated American art collector, is
governed by his purist collector's sensibility. It makes "him impatient of vulgar troubles," and leads "him to live by himself, in a sorted, sifted, arranged
world, thinking about art and beauty and history." Ralph's and Osmond's
lives are "a matter of connoisseurship," and their collector's appreciation
of objets d'art indicate their Europeanized sensibilities. However, in Ralph
Touchett connoisseurship is "an anomaly, a kind of humorous excrescence,
whereas in Mr. Osmond it [is] the keynote, and everything [is] in harmony
with it" (3:376–77). Ned Rosier, moreover, is conceived, and conceives of
the world, entirely through the rhetoric of collection. He admires Isabel
because of "his eye for decorative character, his instinct for authenticity,"
and most especially because he has "a sense for uncatalogued values, for that
secret of a 'lustre' beyond any recorded losing or rediscovering, which his
devotion to brittle wares had still not disqualified him to recognise" (4:105).
However, Pansy Osmond, not Isabel, incites in him an insatiable desire to
collect. After meeting her once he thinks of little else except adding Pansy
to his collection: "[He] thought of her in amorous meditation a good deal
as he might have thought of a Dresden-china shepherdess. Miss Osmond,
indeed, in the bloom of her juvenility, had a hint of the rococo which Rosier,
whose taste was predominantly for that manner, could not fail to appreciate"
(3:90).

When Rosier broaches the subject of Pansy with Madame Merle, he begins
by asserting, " 'I love my things.' " Only in this way can he express his
love for Pansy, exclaiming " 'I care more for Miss Osmond than for all
the *bibelots* in Europe!' " (3:91–92). To make himself more acceptable to
Pansy's father, Rosier does not change his beliefs, his profession, or his
demeanor; considering it the ultimate self-sacrifice, Rosier divests himself
of his collection, which Osmond considers mere bric-a-brac, in the hope
that such an emptying of the self will make room for the treasure he values
most of all—Osmond's daughter.

The degree to which each of these displaced Americans identifies himself
through his collections indicates the degree to which each has lost a "natural
identity" to fall back upon: with neither the innocence and idealism of their
American origins that fuels Henrietta Stackpole's self-possessiveness, nor a
natural place among the cultural landscape of the Old World that invests
Lord Warburton and his sisters with unquestionable national and individual
identities, the expatriated Americans are relegated by their rootlessness and
loss of national/cultural context to a marginal position from which they can

only collect artifacts of a world in which they cannot fully participate. For those with no apparent familial or professional connections, like Gilbert Osmond, collecting artifacts is the structure and content of their lives. As a result, perhaps as a defense against the threat of complete self-loss, they frame Europe as a recondite museum world. They collect its icons and adopt them as self-identifying symbols. They become compulsive collectors, trying to draw within the frames of their identities all that will increase their value— all that enhances a sense of self. Even to women, like Osmond's daughter, Pansy, these collectors assign aesthetic value: Rosier and Osmond consider Pansy as a valuable object, and in their discussion of her each exposes his desire to control her value:

> Osmond stared into the fire a moment. "I set a great price on my daughter."
> "You can't set a higher one than I do," Rosier replies. (4:121)

Women function in the lives of these connoisseurs as art objects. They are as collectible as any other elements of the European cultural landscape, and to Osmond, none is so worthy of collection as Isabel.

We must wonder, then, if James's insistent reference to literary icons—to Turgenev, to Eliot, to Shakespeare—is a defensive move that masks (what James perceives as) the novel's fragile identity. He too is collecting icons from the Old World rather than bringing them to Europe from the New World. Just as Isabel's relation to the Touchett fortune makes her more marriageable, her relation to the women of a rich literary tradition makes her far more attractive as a literary centerpiece. In short, the preface and the novel share a fundamental anxiety that James seems intent upon both allaying and exposing. The anxiety touches on the moral value of the aesthetic consciousness, and the sacrifices that are suitable for such a high degree of aesthetic sensitivity as it participates in the Realist aesthetic of fiction. Morality is central to James and to other Realists; the test of morality is always aesthetic, for morality and art are inseparable. James contends that "the worth of a given subject," is the only measure of morality in literature, and worth can be ascertained by asking, "Is it valid, in a word, is it genuine, is it sincere, the result of some direct impression or perception of life" (3:ix). The Realist's fundamental concern with the morality of art is that it must be true to life and derived from life. James implicitly contrasts himself and Osmond, then, by demonstrating Osmond's essential immoral aesthetic sense, which cares for nothing but to distinguish Osmond from the living world about him, whereas James is concerned with an active interrelation of art and the world.

Ralph understands that Osmond's desire to marry his cousin is not born of greed, but of his passion for accumulation of the very best that nevertheless has no moral grounding: Osmond is "a critic, a student of the exquisite," Ralph maintains, and therefore it would be "natural he should be curious of so rare an apparition" as Isabel (3:393–94). As a rare and valuable curiosity, Isabel is particularly collectible. Osmond fully appreciates Isabel's value: "He was immensely pleased with his young lady; Madame Merle had made him a present of incalculable value. What could be a finer thing to live with than high spirit attuned to softness? . . . This lady's intelligence was to be a silver plate, not an earthen one—a plate that he might heap up with ripe fruits, to which it would give a decorative value"—a plate the value of which he might assume for himself (4:79). And, for a self-conscious art object, which Isabel Archer has become, determination by the man with the greatest aesthetic sense "seemed to assure [Isabel] a future at a high level of consciousness of the beautiful" (4:82). Yet Osmond does not see in Isabel a view into the world from which he has excluded himself; he sees her as an object to be removed from the world.

Isabel, on the other hand, becomes increasingly aware of the moral complexity of the aesthetic consciousness. For example, once she realizes that she has been collected by Osmond, and that the fate of a woman is to be determined by the context of the collection into which she will be placed once married, Isabel acts with greater acumen and responsibility toward her soon-to-be-collected stepdaughter, Pansy. Isabel tries to remain uninvolved in Ned Rosier's attempt to become Pansy's husband because she wishes to remain loyal to her husband (and, one suspects, she realizes that Rosier is an inveterate collector, who finds in Pansy much of what Osmond thought he had found in Isabel). Her reluctance to encourage Lord Warburton to pursue Pansy, on the other hand, stems from an ambivalent fear that her unrequited paramour is not collector enough to fully appreciate the young girl. Isabel understands even before she marries Osmond that women are considered art objects and that Pansy is a most exquisite one: on first seeing Pansy in society, Isabel notes that "Pansy was so formed and finished for her tiny place in the world, and yet in imagination, as one could see, so innocent and infantine. . . . She was like a sheet of blank paper—the ideal *jeune fille* of foreign fiction. Isabel hoped that so fair and smooth a page would be covered with an edifying text" (3:401). Osmond is the ultimate collector, and he has made Pansy into the ideal icon. Like a framed composition, she signifies the proprietary authority of her collector without any self-determining impulses to rival the context in which she is situated. The man who will determine the text that will cover her, at present her father, eventually will be the man with whom she is allied in marriage: an edifying author, it is hoped, who would recognize the literary tradition to which Pansy belongs.

Like Gilbert Osmond, whose wife, daughter, and art collection all signify the aesthetic powers of their collector because they exist and are perceived within the frame of Osmond's identity (Isabel is *his* wife; Pansy *his* daughter; the objets d'art *his* objects), James appropriates the central consciousness of his novel, the characters who attend her, and the plot that they create, as signs of his powers as an author. James's characters must work within his construct and they finally contribute to his *identity* as an author, yet that identity is already partially defined by the philosophy of art and the aesthetic of fiction that James has articulated. While identity is determined by context, it must be the object of perception if it is to be of any value. In other words, James's authorial identity is dependent upon the presence of a reader, of one who will perceive his value. James would not delegate full responsibility for the narrative, therefore, because he would trust no one but himself to colonize the reader: as to his relation with the reader, James says, "I felt no one to be trusted but myself" (3:xix). Even Osmond, who would turn his back on the world and remove his art objects from it, is utterly dependent on the world for his identity and sense of personal worth. Almost in spite of himself, Osmond cares for society most of all: "he was unable to live without it, and [Isabel] saw that he had never really done so; he had looked at it out of his window even when he appeared to be most detached from it. . . . There were certain things [Isabel and Osmond] must do, a certain posture they must take, certain people they must know and not know" (4:198–99). Osmond's self-determination is severely limited, therefore, by his relationship to society. Although "his ambition was not to please the world, but to please himself by exciting the world's curiosity" (4:145), Gilbert Osmond sorely needs the goods that excite that curiosity and he requires onlookers who would evince the sought-after emotions. Isabel is such an article, and Pansy promises to become another. Osmond seeks to determine their identities rigidly because, as his appurtenances, they bear directly upon his sense of himself and on his identity and value in society.

James, on the other hand, worked strenuously to create a relationship with society—his readership—that did not limit him or undervalue him. As author, he did not seclude himself from society, as Osmond did, just to turn readers away once they articulated their desire. James calls himself solicitous: "That solicitude [to the reader] was to be accordingly expressed in the artful patience with which, as I have said, I piled brick upon brick . . . putting for bricks little touches and inventions and enhancements by the way" (3:xix). James presents an image of the author as he supervises the construction of the narrative, interfering in the work of his characters only when he feels the necessity of adding little touches and inventions. Although he denies responsibility for plot, James retains it for the novel's "architecture." And though like Osmond, James sat in his window, he went there to take in all that the world had to offer him, not to flash iconic representations of himself in an effort to excite an interest he would later spurn.

In the determinism that entraps Osmond in his aesthetic greed, therefore, James can find "boundless freedom and . . . 'moral' reference" (3:xi), which James avows can be expressed by narrating the history of individual perception and thereby describing subjective consciousness (James's contribution to the Realist aesthetic). Thus James differentiates himself from Osmond by expressing his belief that the signifier of the greatest aesthetic power is the creation and representation of an Other, not of the self. Osmond wanted Isabel "to have nothing of her own but her pretty appearance"— no ideas, and most important, no character (4:195). James, on the other hand, worries that the central consciousness of his text will have too little character to carry the weight of the narrative. Yet he centers the narrative in her consciousness; he shows us his fictional world through her eyes. Osmond, in contrast, would have her eyes merely reflect his own world, his own creation, his own consciousness. In this sense, James proves a better husband, though no less patriarchal, than Osmond. Intertextuality in the preface emphasizes the relation between self-determination on the one hand, and the aesthetic object's fate of being "created" and "controlled" on the other. James wants his reader to recognize from the outset that Isabel is an aesthetic object, that she will be collected (by a tradition or by a husband), and that her fate is inescapable. Unlike Osmond, he honors the powers of her subjective consciousness, but like Osmond, he composes her within the frame of his own identity.

The paradox of self-determination and determination-by-context in *The Portrait of a Lady* is figured repeatedly in the act of framing. Isabel physically frames herself in doorways more than once, as if she were a compositional element in search of a context. But framing (unlike being framed by another) is, finally, an act of self-assertion, an identification of the self as the perceiving conciousness, which creates through and is created by the act of awareness. In this light, Isabel identifies herself by confronting her own destiny and by electing to explore the full moral complexities of the composition into which she has stumbled. She takes ownership of her fate *as her fate*, just as she told Lord Warburton she must. She returns in the end to Roccanera to exercise the freedom that comes with acceptance of responsibility. She implicitly identifies herself as the architect and not as the passive victim of others' imaginations.

Nothing in this reading of *The Portrait of a Lady* is new, and that is precisely the point: the prefaces in particular and Henry James in general helped establish the terms and the tropes for the readings of his work, and the ways in which we have come to understand literature during and since the modernist era. James relied upon the inessential self—the self that can be revised and altered, by supplementation and change of context—to create an identity both for his reader and for his work. He frames and reframes the work, the reader, and the author repeatedly through the prefaces, and so inaugurates an era that both repelled him and tantalized him (as John Carlos Rowe and Ross Posnock have shown in their studies of James and modernism).

The prefaces are, as Boris Uspensky says all frames are, transitions from the real world of the reader to the world of the narrative, but they are also commitments: the prefaces commit the narratives to yoked states of perpetual creation and consumption; moreover, they commit the reader to a strange marriage with the author, who "pre-reads" the novels and tales, and in the prefaces prepares a critical context for the reader's understanding of them. The novels and tales of the Edition become icons signifying James's identity as an author. The goal of the Edition, James's *vade mecum*, is a colony of Jamesian readers who will idolize the author and valorize his work, a colony of readers who will faithfully keep the master alive through their devotions to his iconic Edition. Thus the reader, like Isabel Archer, is contextualized by the prefaces. The reader is framed by James's act of reading, which he superimposes on the reader. The inside of art is turned outward, then, and the outside pulled inward, with the reader seeing through the creator's eyes while the creator continually provides frames of reference by which the entire world of Henry James's fiction will be known.

Shortly before he died, James acknowledged that few had understood the purpose and plan of either the New York Edition as a whole or of the prefaces in particular. He called the Edition, "a monument (like Ozymandias) which has never had the least intelligent critical justice done to it—or any sort of critical attention at all paid to it."[9] James was disappointed by the paucity of reviews and embarrassed that so few buyers subscribed to the Edition. He had erected a monument to his fine intelligence and, for the most part, it had gone unnoticed. His failure to immediately create a colony of readers contributed to an emotional collapse from which James, at least as an artist, never fully recovered. Yet the history of reading that began soon after James's death is a history of almost cultlike colonization. James's readers have deferred willingly and loyally to the critical and evaluative frames of desire that James left behind, the profound signification of which hovers, like Isabel Archer, above the text and before the reader like a ghostly presence sent to initiate and indoctrinate, to guide the reader through the ado of becoming a Jamesian.

9. Quoted in Edel, *Henry James: The Master: 1901–1916*, 339.

INDEX